# Oldcotes

*The last Mansion built by
Bess of Hardwick*

## Pamela Kettle

MERTON PRIORY PRESS

First published 2000

Published by Merton Priory Press Ltd
67 Merthyr Road, Whitchurch, Cardiff CF14 1DD

ISBN 1 898937 39 7

*To Alan: A Promise Fulfilled*

Printed by Hillman Printers (Frome) Ltd
Handlemaker Road, Marston Trading Estate
Frome, Somerset BA11 4RW

# Contents

When Hardwick's towers shall bow their head,
Nor Mass be more at Worksop said,
When Bolsover's fair frame shall tend,
Like Oldcoates, to its destined end,
When Chatsworth knows no Candish bounties,
Let fame forget this costly Countess.

*Part of Horace Walpole's epitaph to Bess of Hardwick,
written in 1760 in the margin of his copy of Collins's*
Historical Collections of the Noble Family of
Cavendish, *now in the British Library.*

# Preface

Few people have any idea where Oldcotes, the third and last great house to be built by Elizabeth, Dowager Countess of Shrewsbury ('Bess of Hardwick'), was situated. Sadly, no illustration of it has ever been found and perhaps this is the reason why no one has ever attempted to recount its history. Its erection between 1593 and 1599 was a direct result of Bess's purchase of the neighbouring manors of Stainsby, Heath and Oldcotes with the intention of providing a home of his own for her favourite second son William Cavendish during her lifetime.

This third mansion was erected while the construction of the new Hardwick Hall and the extension of the old Hardwick were under way, when the workforce and materials were readily available. The design used for Oldcotes is believed to be one of several submitted by Robert Smythson to the countess for the new Hardwick, to which it bore a remarkable likeness, but on a smaller scale. These drawings are now at the Royal Insitute of British Architects, London.

With only the unsightly electricity pylons to mar our view, we can still gaze from Sutton Scarsdale across the farmland to the site where once stood Oldcotes. The stream flowing in the valley between marks the boundary of the parishes of Sutton and Heath, just as in Bess's time it formed the boundary between the Sutton-en-le-Dale estate of the 1st Earl Scarsdale and her newly acquired manor of Oldcotes.

In recounting its history, it has throughout been my anxious endeavour to use nothing but historical fact, and conscientious research has brought to light much which hitherto has remained obscure. For example, most writers have followed Daniel and Samuel Lysons's statement in 1817 that the ownership of Oldcotes passed to the Pierrepont family by marriage. This was not so: I have established that it was in fact purchased by Robert Pierrepont, 1st Earl of Kingston, from William Cavendish, 3rd Earl of Devonshire.

I should like to express my heartfelt thanks to my husband Alan, who first commenced this project, and whose encouragement has taken me that extra mile in the face of personal adversity. I also extend my thanks to Richard Sheppard of the Trent and Peak Archaeological Unit at Nottingham University, for helping me obtain information on obscure points. As with all my publications, I am indebted to Philip Riden for advice, for information on the Jones family of Courteenhall (Northants.), and for proof-reading. On a more personal note, my thanks are due to Margaret Roberts for typing my various manuscripts. Equal in importance has been the support given to me by the staffs of the Local Studies Library and Derbyshire Record Office at Matlock, the Public Record

Office, John Lilley of Chesterfield Local Studies Library, the Department of Manuscripts and Special Collections, Nottingham University Library, and Nottinghamshire Archives.

Sutton Scarsdale                                                          Pamela Kettle
June 1999

# Acknowledgements

The author and publisher are indebted to the following for permission to reproduce illustrations:

Fig. 1: Derbyshire Archaeological Society.
Figs. 2, 4, 5 and 8 and back cover: Hardwick Hall, The Devonshire Collection (The National Trust). Photographs: Photographic Survey, Courtauld Institute of Art.
Fig. 3: British Architectural Library, RIBA, London.
Fig. 6: Derbyshire Countryside Ltd.
Figs. 7 and 9 and front cover: Devonshire Collection, Chatsworth. Reproduced by permission of the Duke of Devonshire and the Chatsworth Settlement Trustees. Photographs: University of Nottingham.
Figs. 10, 12: Nottingham City Council: Leisure and Community Services: Local Studies Library.
Fig. 13: Crown copyright. NMR.
Figs. 15, 16, 23 and 26: Manvers Collection, University of Nottingham.
Fig. 17: Witt Print Collection, Courtauld Institute of Art, University of London.
Fig. 21: Derbyshire County Library.

# The building of Oldcotes and its ownership by the Cavendishes

## The early history of Oldcotes manor

There are two public places where the name of this manor is perpetuated. One is on the tomb of Elizabeth Hardwick, Countess of Shrewsbury, in Derby Cathedral, where it is named as one of the great houses built by her: 'This most illustrious Elizabeth, Countess of Shrewsbury built the houses of Chatsworth, Hardwick and Oldcotes, highly distinguished by their magnificence'. It also appears in the great hall of Thoresby (Notts.), where it is listed as one of the estates of the Pierrepont family.

Little interest was ever paid to this manor until the time of the 'illustrious Elizabeth', otherwise known as Bess of Hardwick, although its history is much older. In Domesday Book (1086) the manor is referred to as 'Caldecotes'. The name and spelling have changed considerably over the centuries, being known

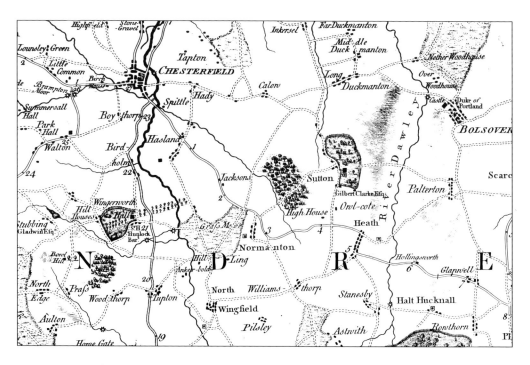

**Figure 1** Extract from P.P. Burdett's map of Derbyshire (1791 ed.), showing 'Owlcotes' (i.e. Oldcotes) and High House a few miles south east of Chesterfield.

as Hulecotes, Ulcote, Owle Cotes, Holecote and Owlcotes, before becoming Oldcotes in the sixteenth century, the name used by Bess and thus preferred here. The modern spelling, Owlcotes, reflects more accurately the meaning of the name, which is 'Owl Cottages' and the confusion with 'Old' is purely dialectical—doubtless due to the broad Derbyshire pronunciation of that word.[1]

Prior to the Norman Conquest it was a manor in the possession of a Saxon named Swain Cilt, and was known as Caldecotes. Following the Conquest it was given by William I to his Norman follower Walter de Aincourt. In 1227 the coheirs of Alan de Handsley conveyed their right to land in Ulecotes to Jocelyn de Havamere, who changed his name to that of the place where he lived and became John de Steynsby. Shortly afterwards it passed into the ownership of the Savages. In 1331 John de Steynesby was sued by the widow of Robert de Savage for her dower, which included 'two ox-gangs of land in Holecote'. This had evidently been conveyed illegally to John de Steynesby. At the same time John claimed free warren in Hardwick and Oulecotes, producing a charter made in favour of his great-great-grandfather, whose heir he was.

Extant is the will, proved on 20 October 1410, of John Savage, who stated that he was the son of Robert Savage:

> John Sauvage of Oulecotes, citizen and clerk of London, 20 March 1408/9. To his brother Sir William a silver cup of weight 13s. 4d. To Sir Robert Scarclif his nephew a silver cup with leopard's feet with a covering of crowns (the coin that is) to the weight of 47s. as bonus. To the fabric fund of the church of All Saints of Heth where he was baptised 40s. To the vicar of the same church 13s. 4d. All lands and tenements which he purchased of John Miriell in Oulecotes are to be sold after his death by his executors, and from the money raised, a chaplain to be provided to celebrate divine service daily for his soul and his father's and mother's souls. To his brother Sir William 100 marks which William holds from him, on condition that William celebrate masses and perform charitable acts for his soul. To John Gaytford his kinsman 80 marks in which Gaytford is bound to him, on condition similar to that required of his brother. £20 to poor heads of household without means of goods or alms, living in the towns or hamlets of Steynesby, Heath, Oulecotes, Sutton, Bolsore, Palterton, Scarcliffe and Nettelworth at the time of his death. Sir William Savage his brother and Sir Robert Scarclif his nephew to be two of the executors.[2]

[1] K. Cameron, *The place-names of Derbyshire* (1959), 262.

[2] *Derbyshire wills proved in the Prerogative Court of Canterbury, 1393–1574* (ed. D.G. Edwards) (Derbyshire Record Society, 26, 1998), 223–4.

In 1432 it was found that William Hardwick of Hardwick gent. held three-quarters of a knight's fee in Oldcotes and at his death in 1495 Roger Hardwick had two bovates of land there. When John Hardwick died in 1507 he held property of John Savage kt of Cheshire as of his manor of Stainsby. So it was that his son, also John Hardwick, a man 'of ancient family, but diminished fortune', came to farm the 400-acre estate which had been held by the Hardwicks since the early fourteenth century.

In a half-timbered manor house, his wife, formerly Elizabeth Leake of Hasland, near Chesterfield, gave birth to four daughters and a son, James, before John her husband died on 29 January 1528, when it was found that land in Heath, Hardwick, Hardstoft, Astwith and Ouldcotes was held by him in the same manner and of the same lord as his father had held it. In his will John directed that his daughters should each receive 40 marks (£26) as a marriage dowry—an impossible amount, as his widow realised, as she struggled to rear her family. His heir was his son James, a minor, and certain lands in Ouldcotes were sold with his wardship as being worth 16s. a year.

After two years, in an effort to improve her financial situation, the widow remarried, but the birth of three more daughters did little to alleviate the situation. Meanwhile, John Hardwick's third daughter Elizabeth followed the custom of her time for children to be brought up by friends or relatives and trained in household management. Thus, Bess, as she became known, joined the London household of Lady Zouche. This lady from Codnor Castle, in mid Derbyshire, was a relative of the Hardwicks and perhaps she chose this young girl as 'the best of the bunch'. Certainly, the training she received in Lady Zouche's household was to prove exceedingly beneficial to Bess in later life.

Numerous books have been written about this illustrious lady and her four husbands,[1] and it is not our purpose here to recount her history. However, the events of life shape the destiny of us all, and so we must outline the story.


## She was determined to be great: he had greatness thrust upon him

The instability of Bess's early life sharpened her acute business instinct. Quick to learn, she realised the only way open to a woman to better her position in those days was by advantageous marriage, and so, following each widowhood,

---

[1] Notably D.N. Durant, *Bess of Hardwick. Portrait of an Elizabethan dynast* (1977), M. Rawson, *Bess of Hardwick and her circle* (1910), E.C. Williams, *Bess of Hardwick* (1959). See also D. Crook, 'Hardwick before Bess: The origins and early history of the Hardwick family and their estate', *Derbyshire Archaeological Journal*, 107 (1987), 41–54.

her remarriage marked a rise on the social ladder.

> Four times the nuptial bed she warm'd
> And every time so well perform'd
> That when death spoil'd each husband's billing
> He left the widow every shilling[1]

Horace Walpole, 1760

In achieving this she was helped by her appearance, for she was of average height, slim with red hair, and although her eyes were small she had great charisma, and men found her witty and attractive. Her six surviving children were all by her second husband, William Cavendish. All four husbands were captivated by her and she was capable of returning their affection. Her last marriage, in the autumn of 1567 when she was in her late thirties, was to one of the wealthiest and most powerful men of that time, namely George Talbot, 6th Earl of Shrewsbury, a widower with four sons and three daughters. Immensely rich and possessed of vast estates in five counties, he owned eight principal residences, two London houses and one in Chelsea. The same age as Bess, he was nearly six feet tall, with a long face, long beard and large melancholy eyes. It was a marriage of convenience from which both parties stood to benefit. The following year the knot was further strengthened by a double wedding, when Gilbert Talbot aged 16 was married to Mary Cavendish aged 12, and Henry Cavendish aged 18 married Grace Talbot who was only eight years old. The lands conveyed in the settlements for these marriages were retained by their parents for their lives, then to the married couples.

The story of the eventual breakdown of the earl and countess's marriage some years later is well documented, but there is no reason to believe that this marriage would not have been as successful as Bess's previous ones, had it not been for circumstances beyond their control. For all the earl was a joyless man, he was intensely loyal to his sovereign, Queen Elizabeth I, and she exploited this advantage to the full, thrusting upon the newly wed pair the enormous responsibility of the custody of the captive Mary, Queen of Scots. This without doubt undermined the Shrewsbury marriage, placing great restrictions on their lives and governing their every movement. By the time the Queen relieved him of his onerous task, the earl had become so embittered towards his wife and her overriding schemes for the advancement of her family, that even the Queen's intervention could not effect a reconciliation.

---

[1] This was not strictly true: her fourth husband did not leave her every shilling.

10

**Figure 2** Elizabeth, Dowager Countess of Shrewsbury ('Bess of Hardwick') in widowhood.

A year before her marriage to William Cavendish in 1547, Bess's brother

James had taken over the Hardwick estates. Although twice married James had no legitimate heirs, and lost money he did not possess in stupid speculation, eventually dying a bankrupt in the Fleet gaol in 1581.

In 1583, when Bess was 56, the earl cut off her allowances, and intercepted revenues from lands made over to her sons William and Charles Cavendish. Bess took refuge at Chatsworth, but Chatsworth was entailed on her eldest son Henry. Unwelcome at any of her husband's residences, she felt virtually homeless, and in this same year she paid £9,500 for the Hardwick lands, buying them in the name of William, her second son, from the Lord Chancellor and the auditor acting for the bankrupt estate of her deceased brother. Meanwhile, relations between the earl and his countess became even more fraught in spite of every attempt by the Queen at reconciliation, and in desperation Bess commenced the restoration and extension of her birthplace Hardwick in 1587.

On the death of the Duke of Norfolk, Shrewsbury succeeded him as Earl Marshal of England, and as such was required to be present at the trial of the Queen of Scots and later at her execution at Fotheringay Castle on 8 February 1587, his duty being to raise his baton to signal the fatal stroke of the axe. It is said that when, after several attempts, the head was finally severed, as the Queen's little Skye terrier crept from beneath her bloodstained skirts, Shrewsbury turned away his head and unashamedly wept. Loyalty to his sovereign had cost him dear; the custody of his captive queen had eaten away his fortune and helped to ruin his marriage. Embitterment towards Bess turned to pure hatred, his health deteriorated rapidly and he died on 18 November 1590, leaving little money but vast possessions.

After several quarrels with Gilbert Shewsbury, his father's heir, Bess got possession of all the properties to which she was entitled under the marriage settlement. Her income was now about £60,000 a year. With Chatsworth entailed to 'my bad son, Henry', the only house she owned outright was Hardwick. Here she resided with her favourite son William, who on 21 March 1581 married Ann Keighley of Keighley (Yorks).

Long before the Earl of Shrewsbury's death, Bess had plans drawn up for a new hall at Hardwick which was to be the setting for 'my jewel, Arbel', the orphaned granddaughter who stood so tantalisingly near the throne as a possible successor to Queen Elizabeth. Life in the old Hardwick Hall became somewhat crowded; William and Ann had a growing family, and workmen were already engaged on the foundations of the New Hall, some residing in the Old Hall. Bess decided William required a home of his own, and with this in mind she purchased from Sir John Savage the adjoining manors of Stainsby, Rowthorne, Heath and Oldcotes.

This is confirmed by entries in the Hardwick household accounts:[1]

*January 18 1593*
Delivered unto Mr William Cavendish the xviij of Januar towards the payment to Mr Savage his lands in Steynesbie and Heath etc ... Two thousand and fyftie pounds.

*27 January 1593*
Edward Savage to Elizabeth, Countess Dowager of Shrewsbury, release of the Titles to the Manors of Stainsbie, Rowthorn, Heathe and Oldcotes in consideration of £3,416 13s. 4d.

*13 March 1593*
Delivered unto Mr William Cavendish to paie unto Mr Savage in full payment of all his lands in Stainsbie and Heathe, thirteen Hundrethe pounds.

Oldcotes being a manor in its own right, with a manor house of some kind, the countess and William decided this would provide a suitable site for a large mansion on similar lines to Hardwick New Hall.

## The construction of Oldcotes

Work at Hardwick Old Hall was completed by 1591, and work on the New Hall took place from 1591 to 1598. Whilst this was in progress, work on the new Oldcotes commenced soon after March 1593. A contract mentions the names of the six principal wallers, who were already employed at Hardwick at the time. They were expected to complete the main structure within eight months, indicating that the building was to be much smaller than Hardwick. The contract was between Elizabeth, Countess of Shrewsbury and William Cavendish of Hardwick, of the one part and Godfrey Plumtree, Reynold Plumtree, Ralph Plumtree, George Plumtree, Robert Ashmore and John Ward of the other.

[1] Chatsworth House, Hardwick MSS.

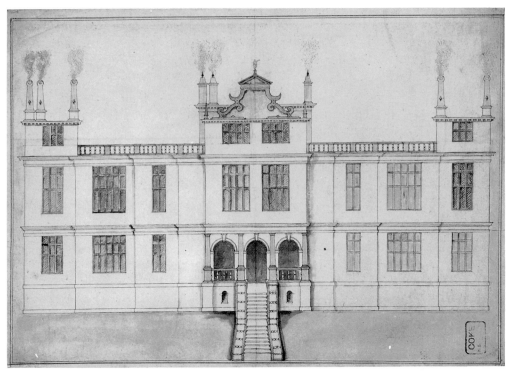

**Figure 3** A drawing in the Smythson Collection at the Royal Institute of British Architects, which may be Robert Smythson's design for Oldcotes.

## The Contract[1]

First the sayde Godfry Renolde Raufe and George Plumtrees Robert Ashmore and John Warde doe for themselves theyre executors and assignes Covenant promise and graunt to and with the saide Countess and William Cavendish theye executors and assignes by theise presents viz. to wale and make all the walls belonging to one house ment and appoynted by the said Countess to be erected and built at Owlcotes in the Countie of Derby from the bottome of the Celler to the top of the roufe and too Turrets above the roufe according to a Plat thereof alreddy drawne whereunto the saide Godfry [etc.] have set theyre hands.

The utter wales of which they Covenant to make too foote Eight inches thick till it come to the highest height, and then to be too foote and a half thick, and to put seven through stones in everie rode and well and

---

[1] *The Building of Hardwick Hall. Part 2. The New Hall, 1591–8* (ed. D. Durant and P. Riden) (Derbyshire Record Society, 9, 1984), pp. lxxvi–lxxvii.

workmanlike to skappell[1] the outside of all the saide wales and Coynes according and like unto the best of the wales of that house which is already built at Owlcotes aforesaide, and likewise to skappell the insides of all the wales in the kychin, and to make the particon wales two foote thick or less as it shalbe thought needful by the Countess and William Cavendish or theyre officers. And the myddle wale to be fowre foote thick and to make all the Rannge, boyling place, too ovins[2] Chymneys dores and steps which rise within the grounde, the saide Countess and William Cavendish fynding all the stone which shalbe by them or theyre officers appoynted to be geven eyther for dores windowes or Chymneys and causing the same to be set at the Costs and Chardges of the Countess and William Cavendish, and of which too ovins aforesaid must be fowre foote wide and the other three foot wide.

Item the said Godfrey [etc.] do Covenant and promise by theise presents after the Parrells in the Chymneys of the said house ar sett, to bring up all the Chymney Conduits to the top of the said wales reddy to be set on the shafts and to parget the Conduits of the sayde Chymneys, and to make the backs of the said Chymneys of fyre stone, and to make good and sufficient archies over all the doors windoes and Chymneys or in any other place that shall happen in the syde wales and to bring up and work all the wales of the saide house strayte and workmanlike.

Item the said Countess and William Cavendish doe Covenant to cause somuch stone Lyme sande and water to be brought and layde forwarde to the saide house as shalbe needfull and Convenyent for the making of the said wales at the costs of the said Countess and William Cavendish and they the said Plumtrees Warde and Ashmore doe Covenant to make all the morter and skaffolds at theyre owne Costs having twentie dozen of hurdells and poles layde by somany as shalbe needful.

Item the said Plumtrees Warde and Ashmore doe Covenant to doe what they can well and workmanlike to worke skappell and fynish all the sayde wales before alhollautide next, and that they will all Contynually worke at the said works untill they have done and finished the same and will doe theyr best too get too or fowre walers more to help them until they have finished and done all the saide wales.

Item the sayde Countess and William Cavendish doe Covenant to paye unto the saide Plumtrees Warde and Ashmore for everie rode of wale aswell the utter wales and Inner wales till they come to the height of

---

[1] To reduce stone to a level surface without smoothing.

[2] In this period ovens were built into the side of the chimneys; not until the late eighteenth century were cast-iron ovens introduced.

twentie foote above the ground which wilbe to the top of the hale roof three shillings fowre pence for every rode of wale and for everie rode of wale above the sayde height fyve shillings, measuring all the Dores, windowes and Chymneys in the sayde wale and in Consideration of the too Turrets above the leads to give them xxxs. more than theyre work shall amount to by measure after the sayde rates, and for making of the too Ovins twentie shillings more, and to paye them at the end of every fortnight somuch as theyre work shall amount to by measure after the rates aforesayde and to measure the utter wales on the outsides thereof. And to lend them the said Plumtree Warde and Ashmoer six beds so long as they shalbe in the sayde works and likewise to lend them three kye from Maye Daye next until Martilmas next and to gyve them a quarter of rye and a strike of Otemeal.

In wytnes whereof the saide parties to theise articles have set theyre hands and Seals the daye and yere first abovewritten. *Marks of Robert Ashmore, John Ward, Raffe Plumtree, Georg Plumtrees, Godfry Plumtrees, Reynold Plumtre.*

From the agreement we can deduce that, like the majority of country houses, Oldcotes was built of local material, in this case sandstone obtained from a quarry close to the site. It would be quarried by Bess's own workforce from Stone Delf, to the north on the Sutton boundary. The stone would be worked on at the quarry so that any surplus weight was removed before being conveyed by horse to the site, and any shortage of stone could be obtained from the Hardwick quarry. Copies of the plan would be handed to the workmen and much of what was built was based on longstanding traditions of craftsmanship, as is clearly demonstrated in the wallers' agreement. There was no architect; Bess and William were firmly in control, while some decisions were left to the man in charge—probably John Ward—who had progressed from a waller at Hardwick to being a mason at Oldcotes. From mid March to mid September the labourers worked from 5 a.m. to 7 or 8 p.m., with breaks of not more than two hours during the day; a shorter day was worked during the winter when they worked from light until dark. The wallers were supplied with six beds and they would use the old house as living accommodation. Although Bess was reckoned as generous to her workforce, the food allowance was rather sparse. The three kine lent from May to Martinmass would provide dairy food. The staple diet seems to have been oatmeal and porridge and oatcakes, but then only the gentry ate wheat flour. Others were forced to content themselves with rye or a mixture of rye and wheat ('blend corn') for bread.

In 1594–7 heavy rains washed away the harvests, bringing famine, starvation and disease; therefore employment at Oldcotes must have proved a god-send.

In times of dearth, bread was made from either beans, oats or peas. Hopefully they were allowed to help themselves to the game on the estate.

It should be noted that these wallers were only engaged to build the walls of this new mansion—they were only responsible for the shell of the house. The labour accounts show all six men briefly at Hardwick in June 1593 and June 1594 with Ward and Ashmore absent until the autumn of 1595, and the four Plumtrees until the summer of 1596.[1] Whether the wallers, even with two or four more to help them, were able to complete the work by All Hallows is not clear. Most contracts contained a clause specifying a completion date but only rarely was it accompanied by a penalty for failure.

The wallers would be followed by a host of other craftsmen—paviours, sawyers, roofers, smiths, joiners, carpenters, plasterers, plumbers, glaziers, mat-makers and painters—all of whom were already employed at Hardwick.

There was no shortage of timber as this area was well wooded. Oak was used for structural purposes because of its strength, durability and natural abundance; ash and elder were used for scaffolding; much of the oak was used unseasoned as it was easier to work and as it dried out it became harder. For floors, doors and panelling it was advisable to use seasoned wood to prevent warping. The principal carpenter selected the right timber for the task from the standing trees, and the felled trees were taken to the building site where the carpenters could work on them and adjustments could be made. The placing of the roof timbers marked the final stage in the erection of the shell and was often the cause of a celebration. Perhaps the following extract from the Countess's household accounts marks such an occasion: 4 May 'Delivered unto my Lady at her going to Oule Coattes Three Pounds, delivered there unto her more is Eleven shillings'. The latter was perhaps a tip for the workmen.

Because of its malleable qualities and freedom from rust, lead was used for roofing, especially flat roofs, and for glazing and rainwater goods. It would be extensively used at Oldcotes as the countess had her own lead mines. Iron was used for a variety of purposes, such as clamps, glazing bars, tools and a vast quantity of nails, and also for artistic fittings such as hinges and firebacks.

At Hardwick the countess had set up a glasshouse for the manufacture of glass during the course of her building; without doubt, Oldcotes glass would come from this source. Plaster was used in large quantities for wall surfaces, ceilings and floors. It was composed of lime and sand, strengthened with chopped straw and hair.

It is disappointing that no record has survived of the names of the various craftsmen involved in the completion of Oldcotes, but we can safely assume

---

[1] *The Building of Hardwick Hall. Part 2*, p. xxvi.

they would be the same men who had been and indeed still were engaged on the work at Hardwick. Perhaps Abraham Smith, a skilled plasterer, was responsible for plastering the walls and ceilings which would be finished off with whitewash made from Crich lime, applied by the plasterers. As he was a skilled plasterer he may have modelled some of the overmantels. The walls of the more important rooms would later be covered with tapestries. Timber was used economically, hence the upper floors would be of lime plaster which was quite traditional in this area.

Bess used her extensive land holdings to secure long-term commitment of her best craftsmen, providing some with rent-free farms. Abraham Smith was one of these and had a 55-acre farm at Ashford-in-the-Water leased to him. He was tied to the Cavendish family from 1589 to 1616.[1]

We are fortunate in being able to trace what became of the six wallers who worked on Oldcotes. Robert Ashmore may be identical with the person of that name who had a house and five acres in the common fields at Edensor, on the Cavendish estate, in 1617.[2] As with all building craftsmen he could not afford to rely entirely on his trade for subsistance and a smallholding or farm was a great help. A John Ward appears at Beighton in 1600, occupying a house, four acres of enclosed land and 10 acres in the common fields.[3] Reynold Plumtree had a house and croft in Heath in 1609 and a farm of 66 acres in Hardstoft.[4]

From an entry in the memorandum book of Arthur Mower of Barlow Woodseats dated 1563 we learn that 'the Countess of Shrewsbury let Moorhall, Barlow, in May 1603 to Humphrey Edmundson who let some of the ground to two or three of the Plumtrees who had been wallers and workmen with the old Countess'.[5]

The chief glazier at Oldcotes would undoubtedly had been Richard Snidall, who later lived in Chesterfield where he had a shop until his death in 1612 when he was still working for William Cavendish.[6]

Unfortunately, while William Cavendish's accounts were very methodical, payments for the building at Oldcotes are merely summarised in his manuscript, e.g. 'pay'd for building at Oldcotes for six weeks ending ye last of April as may apere by my brief of building there'. This 'brief book' has not survived.

[1] *William Senior's survey of the estates of the first and second earls of Devonshire c. 1600–28* (ed. D.V. Fowkes and G.R. Potter) (Derbyshire Record Society, 13, 1988), pp. 118–19.

[2] Ibid., p. 135.

[3] Ibid., p. 8.

[4] Ibid., pp. 21, 26.

[5] C. Jackson, 'Glimpses of mediaeval life, as exemplified in the memorandum book of Arthur Mower', *The Reliquary*, 21 (1880–1).

[6] *The Building of Hardwick Hall. Part 2*, p. lxii.

Although the property belonged to Bess and she clearly took great interest in the erection of the house, the Hardwick records make it clear that it was built for, and the most part at the expense of William: her own accounts only mention the house four times. On 28 March 1593 she delivered to William Cavendish £200 towards the buildings at Oldcotes, and on 4 May her accounts record a payment of £3 'to my La: at her goinge to Oule Coates', plus a further 40s., which may have been tips for the workmen. There are other gifts to William of £100 for Oldcotes on 20 May 1593 and 7 April 1599.[1] In August and September 1599 the accounts record a payment 'To the Joyners for Oldcotes for iii days of work in making a peece of frame for the table in the lowe Great Chamber'.[2] William's own personal account books do not start until 1597, in which year there are payments for £190 for building repairs at Oldcotes, which make it clear that the main work had already been done.[3]

To obtain timber of great lengths for beams must have posed a problem. A letter from Bess's half-sister Elizabeth Wingfield written from Mercaston to her niece Mary, Countess of Shrewsbury, dated 17 October 1597 states: 'There was a great beam fell at Oldcotes whiche bracke 2 others and much shaked the walles but no man hurt, but some a little bruised'.[4] Thus showing that accidents did happen.

The last item in respect of Oldcotes in Bess's accounts reads: '6th November 1600 given to Mr Good at his matting at the Oldcotes of a gallerie'.[5] Mr Good had woven the reed matting to cover the floor of the gallery. This is known as 'Hardwick Matting', and can be seen in use at the Hall at the present time.

The tradition of the countess's death synchronising with heavy frost which stopped the workmen at Oldcotes can have no foundation, for Oldcotes was finished by 1600 and the countess did not die until 1608. Ford's *History of Chesterfield* (1839) refers to another Hardwick tradition, namely that:

> this singular woman, being provoked by a splendid mansion, which the Suttons[6] had recently erected within view of her windows, declared she would build a finer dwelling for the owlets, whence Owlcots or Oldcotes. She kept her word, more truly perhaps than she intended for Oldcotes has since become literally a dwelling for the owls; the chief part of it is in

---

[1] M. Girouard, *Robert Smythson and the architecture of the Elizabethan era* (1966), p. 139, citing Chatsworth House, Hardwick MS 7, ff. 55, 58, MS 8, f. 48.

[2] Chatsworth House, Hardwick MSS.

[3] Girouard, *Robert Smythson*, p. 139, citing Hardwick MS 10(a).

[4] Lambeth Palace, Shrewsbury Papers, vol. 706, f. 35.

[5] Chatsworth House, Hardwick MSS.

[6] i.e. the Leeke family of Sutton.

ruins, and the rest is converted into a farm-house.[1]

This does not refer to the present ruined Sutton Hall which dates from 1724–8, but to 'a new dwelling house' erected by Francis Leeke in about 1595, known as Sutton House, which was certainly smaller than Oldcotes.[2] This goes to prove that we should not automatically discount local legend, as sometimes there is an element of truth.

William Senior's plan of Oldcotes of 1609[3] marks a house on the estate which appears to be purely conventional and not an accurate representation of Bess's mansion. He shows a seven-bay building, only two storeys high, with alternating bays projecting on the south elevation, each with a gabled roof. By contrast, an estate map of 1659, revised in 1688,[4] shows a much more imposing three-storey house with a main south elevation of seven bays with turrets at either end and a central tower. Vertical lines between the windows appear to indicate that there were breaks in the elevation between each bay. All these features are strikingly similar, with one important exception, to those shown in one of a group of anonymous drawings by Robert Smythson which appear to have been prepared at the time he was employed by Bess at Hardwick and may have been rejected schemes for the New Hall there.[5] The arrangement of windows and turrets is broadly similar and there are breaks in the elevation between each bay, but Smythson's drawing is for a two-storey house. If this design was the one chosen for Oldcotes, either the scheme was enlarged between conception and construction, or a third storey was added at a later date. Senior's sketch appears to be a rather half-hearted attempt to represent the same building, since the number of bays matches the Smythson drawing and the later estate map, but instead of showing the Renaissance façade of Smythson's design Senior has drawn an elevation that looks more like a large farmhouse, with gables rather than turrets. The terrier accompanying the map[6] mentions the 'new and ould halls, Courts and Cowepasture' at Oldcotes, the old hall being the the earlier house on the site, the home of the Hardwicks and before them the Savages, which remained standing to the south-east of the new hall after Bess had completed her work at Oldcotes.

[1] *The history of Chesterfield* (1839), p. 455.

[2] P. Kettle, *Sutton Scarsdale's Story. Part 1. The Leekes of Sutton* (1988), p. 30.

[3] Chatsworth House, reproduced here by kind permission of the Duke of Devonshire and the Trustees of the Chatsworth Settlement.

[4] Nottingham University, Ma 2P 238.

[5] Girouard, *Robert Smythson*, pp. 140–1.

[6] *William Senior's Survey*, pp. 17–18.

# William Lord Cavendish, 1st Earl of Devonshire: 'His Mother's Favourite'

William Cavendish was knighted in 1580, when he was thirty years of age, and on 21 March 1582 he was married to Anne Keighley, daughter and heir of Henry Keighley of Keighley (Yorks.). Their entire married life was spent living with his mother, first at Chatsworth and later at Hardwick Old Hall. They had three boys and three girls: Gilbert, William, Frances, Mary, Elizabeth and James.

Both William and Anne frequently conveyed bags of money for the countess on their journeys to London: this money was provided by Bess for William to carry out business transactions on her behalf. They had a town house in Holborn and from here they were able to visit the Court and return to Derbyshire with all the news and gossip so welcome to the countess.

Old Hardwick, in spite of its extension, had its problems as it became somewhat overcrowded and noisy. There was much hammering and banging and comings and goings in connection with the New Hall in process of erection. The countess and her orphaned granddaughter Arbella, with their retinue of servants, occupied one part of the house, while William and Anne and their growing family of children and servants had their own apartments. Small wonder that on 4 October 1597 the countess and Arbella moved into the new Hardwick before it was completed.

There must have been times when Anne gazed longingly across the valley towards their own new mansion in course of erection at Oldcotes. Occasionally she must have ridden over with William to inspect its progress and yearned for its completion, which would free her from the constraining influence of her mother-in-law. But she was destined never to reside at Oldcotes. Cruel fate decreed that she should die soon after the birth of their youngest child, James. Instead, on a bitterly cold day in February 1598, the sad cortège bearing Anne wound its way from Hardwick to Ault Hucknall church for burial.

We are told that in Bess's new drawing room were two childrens' chairs.[1] These were for her son William's motherless children, Gilbert the eldest and young William, then aged seven; any younger children would have to sit on one of the many stools.

James Starkey had joined the household in 1593 as household chaplain and tutor to these children, whom he taught in a room called the Nursery. As time went by he became dissatisfied by William's meanness and left his service in 1601 to move to London.

On 29 March 1599 Bess's accounts record a payment of £100 for 'the full

---

[1] Durant, *Bess of Hardwick*, p. 197.

**Figure 4** William Cavendish, 1st Earl of Devonshire, second son of Bess and William Cavendish.

fenyshing' of Oldcotes.[1] Possibly William and his family occupied Oldcotes before this date. Much of the furniture would come from Old Hardwick and surplus stock from elsewhere. Even William must have found it a refuge and an escape from the demands of his mother.

Always his mother's favourite, William's education at Eton and Cambridge followed by a period at Gray's Inn studying law made him exceedingly useful to Bess in the management of her estates and business interests, so that he became in effect his mother's shadow, hers to command, and by temperament he was content to do her bidding. With advancing years, she, for her part, increasingly appreciated his usefulness, loyalty and devotion, and made him her chief heir. Following the deaths of his wife and James the youngest child, William suffered further personal sorrow in the death of their eldest son Gilbert, 'a young man of incomparable parts', who died young, having written a very ingenious book entitled *Horae Subjectivae. Observations and Discourse etc.*[2] Of their three daughters only Frances survived. Mary and Elizabeth both died young.

It has proved impossible to ascertain how much time during his widowhood William Cavendish actually spent at Oldcotes, which was only two miles from Hardwick, and if summoned there by his mother he was obliged to go. Therefore he may have preferred to remain at Old Hardwick.

In 1597 Arbella, Bess's orphaned granddaughter and only child of her daughter Mary and her husband Charles Stuart, a princess of the blood, had been banned from Court by Queen Elizabeth for her arrogant behaviour towards the Queen's other ladies, and sent back to Hardwick with strict instructions to her grandmother to keep a close watch on her. After Bess had

[1] Chatsworth House, Hardwick MS 8, f. 47.

[2] W. Kennet, *Memoirs of the Family of Cavendish* (1708).

vented her wrath upon her she compelled her to sleep on a bed in her room, a restriction which must have added to Arbella's resentment and hardened her determination to escape from Hardwick at all costs.[1]

A letter from the countess to Sir Robert Cecil shows her great anxiety:

**Figure 5** Arbella Stuart.

> Arbella is so wilfully bent that she hath made a vow not to eat or drink in this house at Hardwick or where I am, 'til she hear from Her Majesty so that for the sake of the preservation of her life, I am enforced to suffer her to go to Oldcotes two miles from here. I am wearied of my life. and earnestly pray you to send Sir Henry Bronker hither. 15th Feb. 1603.[2]

An entry in William's accounts notes that he 'lay'd forth at Oldcotes in a week ended 27th Feb. (Sunday) according to a bill 27s. 9d. being payment for provisions for the house whilst my Lady Arbel and my Mr stayed there'.[3] This gives the impression that the family as such was not in residence and the mansion was probably in the care of a skeleton staff of servants.

Unfortunately, the only consolation Bess received from the Queen and Cecil was the suggestion that William should take some of the burden off his mother's shoulders. The state of Bess's health prevented William doing this and at the same time it was noted that 'Mr William Cavendish being such a weak man for such a purpose and of little love and respect here' was totally unsuitable, and there was no-one else in the area sufficiently responsible to supervise Arbella. However, on 24 March 1603 Queen Elizabeth died and was succeeded by James VI of Scotland, who became James I of England. Arbella's previous behaviour had, as her grandmother realised, ruined any chance she

---

[1] Like her grandmother, Arbella has attracted considerable attention from popular biographers; the following account draws on D.N. Durant, *Arbella Stuart. A rival to the Queen* (1978), E. Cooper, *The life and letters of Lady Arabella Stuart* (1866); E.T. Bradley, *Arabella Stuart* (1889); B.C. Hardy, *Arbella Stuart* (1913); P.M. Handover, *Arbella Stuart* (1957).

[2] F. Broadhurst, 'Elizabeth Hardwycke, Countess of Shrewsbury, A.D. 1520–1608', *Derbyshire Archaeological Journal*, 30 (1908), p. 225.

[3] Chatsworth House, Hardwick MSS.

**Figure 6** Bess of Hardwick's monument in All Saints', Derby.

24

may have had to the succession, but 'cousin James', in sympathy for her, ordered her to be removed from Hardwick to the care of the Earl of Kent at Wrest Park (Beds.). After a short time Arbella persuaded James to release her, and as his only English relative she secured a place at Court in attendance on his wife Queen Anne.

Meanwhile, Oldcotes awaited a mistress. After six years of widowhood, William found a suitable bride. Elizabeth Wortley was the widow of Sir Richard Wortley of Wortley (Yorks.), who died in 1603. She had borne him ten children, so she must have been at least 35 by the time she wed William Cavendish. The marriage must have taken place in 1603–4 and she brought her youngest child, a daughter Sara Ann, with her when she came to reside at Oldcotes. Some lands at Beighton were settled on Elizabeth as her jointure and therefore William would have an interest in them during her lifetime.

In the spring of 1605 Arbella obtained from King James the useful gift of a patent for a peerage with the name left blank. Her uncle William may have lacked personality but he was by far the most selfish and grasping of Bess's brood. Seizing this opportunity, in April 1605 he left Derbyshire for London to stay at his Holborn house and his brother-in-law, Gilbert Shrewsbury, was informed that 'Mr Cavendish is come to Court and waits hard upon Lady Arbella for his barony'. William became Baron Cavendish of Hardwick. The cost of it (around £2,000) was paid by his mother. In a matter of this sort, money had to be freely spent, and William hated to part with his cash. Bess, who still held firmly to the purse strings, paid willingly because she knew the value of a title for her dynasty. It also brought Arbella back into the old lady's favour; she was allowed to visit her, and returned to court with Bess's gift of £300 and a gold cup. Sir Francis Leeke, with his ear to local gossip, informed Gilbert Shrewsbury that Arbella had visited her grandmother.

Animosity frequently existed between neighbouring gentry, and such was the case between the Leekes of Sutton and the Cavendishes at Hardwick. The Leekes curried favour with Gilbert, 7th Earl of Shrewsbury, Bess's son-in-law, with whom she had quarrelled following the death of his father, her husband. A prime example is a letter dated 6 July 1605 written by Francis Leeke to Gilbert: 'Baron Cavendish's wife [Elizabeth] is very sick at Oldcotes and there have been cross words between her and the Dowager Countess of Shrews-bury'.[1]

But even Bess must have rejoiced when a few months later Baroness Cavendish gave birth to a son John. This much loved son, known as Sir John Cavendish, was created a Knight of the Bath at the Coronation of Charles I. He

---

[1] College of Arms, Talbot Papers.

died soon afterwards on 3 March 1625 aged 19, and was buried at Edensor near Chatsworth.

Sir Francis Leeke, gazing from a window of Sutton House across the valley to Oldcotes, writes tantilisingly to Gilbert, Earl of Shrewsbury, on 11 October 1607 that: 'He is too ill to attend the marriage of Sir William Willoughby's son and heir and Mistress Ann Wortley at Oldcote',[1] thus implying that he would be unable to convey any gossip regarding the occasion. Ann, Elizabeth's youngest daughter by Sir Richard Wortley, would probably be about twelve years of age at the time.

In January 1608 Bess realised she was dying. Her tomb in All Hallows' church, Derby, was ready for her, and she was ready for it, but death was not to come quickly. William was a frequent visitor, riding over almost daily from Oldcotes. He was the only company she desired and her thoughts were constantly fixed on him. Aware of the limitations of this favourite son, she endeavoured to guide him for a future without her, for with him lay the foundation of the dynasty she had striven to create. The arranged marriages of two of his children were to go ahead irrespective of her imminent death. It is doubtful if it would have surprised her had she known that during this time William had arranged for all her cattle and sheep in South Yorkshire to be driven down to him upon her death. Death claimed her on 13 February 1608; her exact age none knew. So passed, in the words of her son-in-law the Earl of Shrewsbury, 'a lady of great years, great wealth and of great wit'.

The breath was scarcely out of Bess's body before all her children, stepchildren and grandchildren were squabbling over her property, and the most grasping and callous of them all was her favourite son, William, the one person in the world to whom she had at times been weakly indulgent. Before the will was even opened, however, William had taken possession of Hardwick, seized all the sheep and cattle on her estate, and behaved in such a rude and overbearing manner to his assembled relatives that the Shrewsburys could suffer him no longer and hastily returned to Sheffield.

It was some time in early May before her disembowelled and embalmed remains, sealed in wax and in a lead coffin, left the great chamber at Hardwick for All Hallows' church, Derby.

Meanwhile, Lord Cavendish, in accordance with his late mother's wish, had two weddings to accomplish. William, Lord Cavendish's heir (following the death of his older brother Gilbert), was now eighteen years old. He was knighted on 7 March and was to be married to Christian Bruce aged twelve. Due to the death of the countess the marriage could not take place at either

---

[1] College of Arms, Talbot Papers. The heir was Sir Rotherham Willoughby of Wollaton (Notts.).

Oldcotes or Hardwick and so London was the obvious choice. The following letter refers to this union:[1]

*To Gilbert, 7th Earl of Shrewsbury, 10 April 1608*

May 6. Wee could not omitt to advertise yr Lordship of an accident that will be soe welcome to you as that Mr Wm. Cavendish hath gotten a good wife whoe was this Sonday in the morning married to my Lo. Kinloss, his daughter; the matter hath been soe secretly carried out as it was never heard of, of any, till it was donne, and for me I thinke I was the last, for at my goinge to Whitehall after dinner, the Queen told me of it, and sayes that in the morning John Elvaston asked her leave to goe to the Weddinge which she could not believe till she heard it confirmed by more certainty; the Queene hears that Elvaston and it is thought my La. Arbella were the match makers and that Elvaston hath five or six hundred pounds, that the wench is a pretty red headed wench, and that her portion is seaven thousand pounds, and she heares the youth first refused her and my Lo. of Cavendish tolde him Kinloss was well favoured by the Queene, and if her refused it he would make him the worse by an hundred thousand pound; but I am sure the Queene is far from being pleased with all nowe it is done. and so with our service to yr. Lo. and my La. wee rest.

> Yr Lordships affectionate
> Son and daughter
> to command.
> ARUNDELL, ARUNDELL.

The Earl of Arundell was married to Alethea, daughter and co-heiress of Gilbert, Earl of Shrewsbury, and grand-daughter of Bess. As his uncle Charles Cavendish remarked at the wedding dinner, 'Alas, poor Wylkyn, he desired a woman ready grown, they were bedded together to his great punishment some two hours'. It is unlikely that the marriage was consummated during those two uncomfortable hours, for part of the deal appears to have been that the bridegroom was allowed to keep his freedom and amuse himself until his wife could bear children. Christian Bruce, whilst being a pretty red-headed wench, was only twelve years old, and hence Wylkyn at first refused her. In fact James I made her dowry up to £10,000. Later that same year William's daughter Frances Cavendish, aged 15, was married to William Maynard, subsequently

[1] F. Brodhurst, 'The Devonshire–Bruce marriage', *Notts. & Derbys. Notes & Queries*, 6 (1898), p. 142.

Lord Maynard.

Bess's will held few surprises for her three sons. Her eldest, 'my bad son Henry', inherited Chatsworth, but its contents she left to William. Unfurnished it was of little use to Henry, and in 1610 he sold it to William for £8,000. Charles, her third son, already had his own home at Stoke Hall which Bess had purchased in 1573, and prior to her death he bought Bolsover and Welbeck from his friend and brother-in-law Gilbert, 7th Earl of Shrewsbury. William, as anticipated, inherited Hardwick and, most important of all, he was her residuary legatee. He was now an extremely wealthy man and the sole owner of all the Cavendish mansions named on his mother's tomb.

In her will she clearly states that:

> As she built Chatsworth, Hardwick and Olcotes and furnished the same, now to son William and grandson William is entailed all stuff at Hardwick and Oldcotes. All who became entailed to have special care to preserve them from wett, mooth and other hurte or spoile.

> To her grandson William Cavendish she left a cup of Lapis Lazarus with cover garnished with gold enamel as an heirloom to go with Hardwick

> To her grandson James Cavendish (son of William) £1,000 (with interest at 20 nobles in the hundred) when 20, to be paid as one sum.

> To Frances Cavendish (daughter of William), £1,000 (ditto) when 18, to be paid as one sum.

James never lived to inherit as he died young. His other two sisters (Mary and Elizabeth) were not mentioned in the will, and so they must have died before 27 April 1601, the date of Bess's will.

## The Survey of Oldcotes taken by William Senior in 1609

Immediately after their mother's death William and Charles Cavendish commissioned William Senior to survey their respective estates.[1] The choice of William Senior for this work may well have been due to William's choosing the widow Elizabeth Wortley as his second wife. In 1600 Senior had surveyed Beighton and Birley in north east Derbyshire for Sir Richard Wortley, therefore

---

[1] *William Senior's Survey.*

it is feasible that Cavendish was introduced to Senior through this family link.

The book of surveys accompanying the maps includes the Beighton and Birley survey; this may signify that these lands had formed part of Elizabeth Wortley's jointure on her marriage to William Cavendish and would pass back to the Wortley heir on her death.

A close study of Senior's map enables the reader to establish certain details regarding this manor at this date. A gated road (the modern Shire Lane) separates Shepherds Closes from Oldcotes; there is a gated entrance to Oldcotes at the Green, and a further gate along this road at the junction of Oldcotes with the manor of Sutton Scarsdale. Shepherds Closes is divided into fields of varying acreage and let to the inhabitants of Heath. The farm now known as 'High House' did not exist in 1609, but there are five cottages on the periphery of the Closes, three on the southern boundary of the Closes in the occupation of John Marshall, Frances Roberts and Widow Fox. Three more cottages (denoted as two buildings) border on Shire Lane near the Sutton boundary, which are in the tenure of James Hallam.

The terrier accompanying the map described Oldcotes as follows:

*A perfecte survey of Owldcote belonging to the right honorable William Lord Cavendishe: Taken by William Senior 1609 according to the statute, viz. 16½ feete to the pole 40 poles to a rood and fower Roodes to an acre*

|  | a. | r. | p. |
|---|---|---|---|
| the newe and ould halls, Courts and Cowepasture | 52 | 0 | 10 |
| long medowe | 08 | 3 | 20 |
| Jillian Holme | 09 | 0 | 00 |
| Coat close and wood | 14 | 2 | 20 |
| the ould house fould gardine and white crofte | 49 | 3 | 00 |
| Coweclose wood | 18 | 1 | 00 |
| Calf crofte | 1 | 1 | 00 |
| roughe close | 67 | 1 | 00 |
| the Greene | 7 | 3 | 20 |
| stone delf | 00 | 3 | 00 |
| the Riddings | 19 | 3 | 00 |
| Coweclose medowe | 14 | 3 | 00 |
| Willinsons medowe | 12 | 3 | 00 |
| Hawley close | 01 | 0 | 20 |
| two Scowryes | 05 | 0 | 39 |
| Smithies medowe | 06 | 1 | 16 |
| horse close | 09 | 0 | 00 |

| | | | |
|---|---:|---:|---:|
| two Hawblins | 28 | 1 | 20 |
| Broadfeelds | 50 | 0 | 00 |
| peartre feeld | 35 | 0 | 00 |
| Breaks | 9 | 3 | 30 |
| Keke Leys | 18 | 1 | 10 |
| | | | |
| The totall of Owldcoates | 438 | 1 | 5 |

*Shepherds Closes*

| | | | |
|---|---:|---:|---:|
| 2 in Robert Watkinsons tenure the younger | 26 | 1 | 00 |
| 2 in Robert Watkinsons tenure of Brampton | 11 | 2 | 00 |
| his long Shepherds close | 17 | 1 | 20 |
| a close and 3 cottages in James Hallam tenure | 13 | 2 | 20 |
| 2 closes in Coopers tenure | 09 | 3 | 20 |
| Robert Frocks close | 04 | 1 | 13 |
| Plumtrees Close | 11 | 0 | 00 |
| Williams Woods Close | 04 | 1 | 13 |
| Slacks close | 10 | 3 | 10 |
| John Marshall howse croft & 2 closes | 08 | 2 | 20 |
| Clothall | 03 | 2 | 20 |
| Mustie yate | 04 | 2 | 35 |
| Gorse close | 04 | 0 | 25 |
| Watlyne poole | 01 | 0 | 15 |
| Frances Roberts howse and close | 01 | 0 | 8 |
| the laine | 03 | 1 | 20 |
| widowe Foxes howse and garden | 00 | 0 | 24 |
| | | | |
| The totall of shepherds closes containethe | 135 | 3 | 23 |

## At last: an Earldom

For some unknown reason Lord Cavendish expended a considerable amount on Hardwick, for between 1608 and 1612 £1,163 5s. 6d. was spent on the New Hall and a north wing added to the Old Hall. The accounts are entered in a book kept by John Ballechous (alias Painter) which has since disappeared. It is not known whether William did this before or after he and his wife Elizabeth and their young son John vacated Oldcotes for Hardwick. Plasterwork ceilings in the gallery and similar ceilings at Hardwick may have been part of the undocumented alterations carried out. William also engaged Rowland Lockey to paint

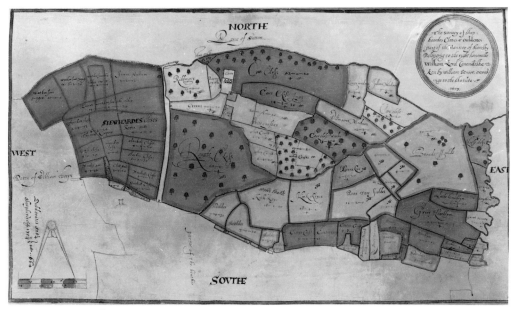

**Figure 7** William Senior's plan of Shepherds Closes and Oldcotes, part of the manor of Stainsby, belonging to William Lord Cavendish, 1609.

30 pictures, chiefly family portraits.

It is known that James I upbraided Cavendish for his meanness towards his son and heir and his wife Christian. Hence it may well be that Oldcotes became their residence and home to their young family. In 1618 Cavendish paid 'the canny Scot' (James I) £10,000 for the title Earl of Devonshire or Devon, in the certain knowledge that his late mother would have wholeheartedly approved. This was a title formerly held by the Courtenay family who, unlike the Cavendishes, had an estate in Devon. The earldom in no way changed William from the acute businessman he was, for what mattered most was his wealth and the Cavendish inheritance—these were more important than duties at Court. Under his shrewd direction the wealth accumulated. He was the foremost magnate of his day to invest heavily in trading companies abroad. Around this time his troublesome niece Arbella died imprisoned in the Tower (1615) while he was spending on average £2,500 a year on speculations in Russian trade, the East and West Indies and America. Gracious living was never one of William's weaknesses. All his account books show how profitably the Devonshire inheritance was managed.

William Cavendish, 1st Earl of Devonshire, died at Hardwick on 3 March 1626 aged 74, and chose to be buried with his elder brother Henry (who had predeceased him in 1616) in Edensor church close to Chatsworth. On the huge monument he appears in a shroud with his face exposed, and Henry is represented as a skeleton on a straw mat. A central inscription is held by an angel with a trumpet and the whole capped by a large broken pediment.

## Sir William Cavendish, 2nd Earl of Devonshire

*'The weak point in every dynasty lies in succession,*
*and the House of Cavendish was no exception'*

Young Wylkyn was only eight years old when his mother died in 1598, but later events proved how clearly he remembered her and his deceased brothers and sisters. He would have been about 14 years of age when his father remarried *c.* 1603–4. Nothing is known of his early education following the resignation of James Starkey as tutor in 1601. His father Lord Cavendish, by now a distinguished courtier and no mean scholar himself, became concerned about his heir's lack of learning. In his search for a suitable tutor for his son he sought the advice of the Principal of Magdalen College, Oxford, who recommended a young member of the college, one Thomas Hobbes who had just taken his bachelor's degree. Thus commenced the great philosopher's connection with the Cavendishes, which was to continue with intermissions throughout his long life. Hobbes was only twenty at the time, and William, although two or three years his junior, was already married, so the relationship to his charge was that of companion rather than tutor.

Lord Cavendish, having lately remarried, begrudged the money required to establish the young couple becomingly, so that James I considered it his duty to exercise his personal influence on their behalf. It is highly probable that Oldcotes became their home, although in view of the bride's tender age the marriage was for several years a mere form, and for some time longer the young Sir William (the King had knighted him a year after his marriage), was for all practical purposes a bachelor.

To begin with, study played a small part in his life and he spent time diligently sowing his wild oats, while Hobbes endeavoured to raise money to meet his creditors. But this way of life ended in 1610, when the two friends, tutor and pupil, set out on the Grand Tour of Europe. They visited France, Germany and Italy, and young William acquired a knowledge of foreign languages and affairs which later made him a useful appendage at the English Court. During his absence Christian would be trained in the art of household management and the intricacies of Court life, in addition to continuing her own education.

On returning from the Grand Tour, the young couple resumed life together as married adults. Their first child, William, was born in 1617 when the father

**Figure 8** William Cavendish, 2nd Earl of Devonshire.

was 27 and Christian was 21. He was followed by a second son Charles and a daughter Anne. There is every reason to believe that Oldcotes would be the background of these children's lives, although it is impossible to be certain of the part played by Oldcotes in the lives of the Cavendish family at this time. With two mansions at Hardwick it would have been possible for both families to have maintained adequate households there, and there was also Chatsworth as an additional residence. It was usual for such families to move around their various houses, and certainly Oldcotes remained one of them.

Meanwhile young Lord Cavendish was proving to be a man of many parts. Not only was he a linguist, but he was deeply versed in history and statecraft, and a patron of the arts and of learning. According to Hobbes his house was an adequate substitute for a university. From 1619 he shared the office of Lord-Lieutenant of Derbyshire with his father, and in 1621 he was elected MP for the county.

Aware of his father's great wealth and his future inheritance Lord Cavendish was a big spender; he became the recognised leader of fashion, and his polished manners and outlook endeared him to James I. Some saw him as a spendthrift, a brawler and a rake, who was easily at home at King James's corrupt Court. He contracted huge debts during his father's lifetime through his excessive gallantry and extravagance. After his father's death in 1626, when he succeeded to the title Earl of Devonshire, he continued to live beyond his means, so much so that he frittered away his father's vast fortune, and in 1627 a bill was introduced in the House of Lords to enable him to sell some of his entailed estates in order to pay his enormous debts. However, he did not live to reap the benefits. 'Excessive indulgence and good living' was given as the cause of his death, which occurred at his splendid London house in Bishop's Gate (on the site of the present Devonshire Square). He died on 20 June 1628 at the early age of 38. He had held the title for a mere two years and was buried in his grandmother's vault in All Hallows' church, Derby. They must have made strange bedfellows!

Visitors to Ault Hucknall church gaze on the magnificent tomb of Ann Cavendish (née Keighley) and presume it was erected by her grieving husband Sir William Cavendish, but they are mistaken. It was in fact erected by her spendthrift son, the 2nd Earl William, who was only a lad of eight when his mother died, and by 1628 was the sole survivor of her six children. The Latin inscription (probably composed by Hobbes) when translated reads:

> In this tomb, under the figures of Modesty, Prudence, Love, Obedience and Piety and of the subsidiary and guardian virtues, are placed and preserved the ashes of the most excellent of women, Ann Keighley, daughter of Henry, of Keighley, in the county of York, Knight. She married the exalted nobleman William Cavendish knight of Chatsworth (afterwards raised to the Earldom of Devonshire) and bore him three sons Gilbert, William and James, and as many daughters, Mary, Elizabeth and Frances. James, the youngest, sleeps beside his mother. William, Earl of Devonshire and Lord Cavendish of Hardwick, the heir and now only survivor, who wishes to preserve at the same time the memory of his dearest mother and brothers and sisters had this monument made. 1628.

> She died in the month of February in the year of our salvation MDXCVIII

Dying shortly after erecting this monument, William Earl of Devonshire left Christian, his 32-year-old widow with three young children and a vast number of debts.

## The Dowager Countess of Devonshire and her son William, the 3rd Earl

*'A wise and witty lady who nursed the*
*properties back to financial solvency'*

Countess Christian realised that retrenchment was essential. She felt she could no longer afford to employ Hobbes as tutor to her children, and to save expense she undertook to educate them herself. Having obtained the wardship of her eldest son William, now the ten-year-old Earl of Devonshire, she set about mending his estates. The pretty red-headed wench had grown into a women of thirty who was witty, and extremely capable. Of the thirty lawsuits, the result of her late husband's extravagances, she won every one. In 1631 she was wise enough to recall Hobbes to tutor the young earl in logic, rhetoric, astronomy,

34

**Figure 9** Christian, Countess of Devonshire, with her children.

law and other subjects. She herself seeking to imbue him with 'all such opinions as should incline him to be a good Christian, a good subject and a good son'.

Three years later Hobbes accompanied the earl, now aged 17, on the Grand Tour of Europe, as he had done his father before him. Although the lands disentailed by Parliament did not produce sufficient to pay all the creditors, by her prudent husbandry and her brother's advice, Christian gradually got things to rights.

William, 3rd Earl of Devonshire, was greatly interested in science and literature, and so his years of travel with Hobbes must have been most beneficial. On his return his mother made over to him the family's great Derbyshire houses. In 1639, when he was 22, he married 19-year-old Elizabeth Cecil, daughter of the Earl of Salisbury.

Two years later we find negotiations were afoot to sell Oldcotes. This formed part of the plan to make savings in order to retain and maintain Hardwick and Chatsworth, and was hardly surprising in view of the number of times the manor of Oldcotes must have been in the occupation of 'caretakers'.

The Cavendish motto is 'Cavendo Tutus', a play on words that means 'Safe by being cautious', and William, guided by his mother, took it thoroughly to heart. He did not take up arms during the Civil War, but he did subscribe handsomely to the King's cause. He considered that his duty was to the house of which he was head, for he chose the unheroic course of exile rather than arms. His younger brother Charles died fighting for King Charles I, aged 23.

When Christian found there was insufficient space for her proposed monument in the chapel at the east end of All Hallows' church, Derby, she obtained permission to extend the chancel southwards. The monument consisted of a heavy canopy over almost life-size figures of her late husband and herself, with busts of their children on the exterior supporting columns. It was later removed to Chatsworth. Christian, Dowager Countess of Devonshire did not die until 1674 and was buried in the Dowager Countess of Shrewsbury's tomb in All Hallows' church, Derby. Her gallant son Charles was reburied her with her that same year.

# Oldcotes in the time of the Pierreponts

## The purchase of Oldcotes by Robert Pierrepont, 1st Earl of Kingston

By 1640 Robert Pierrepont was one of the richest men in England. Educated at Oriel College, Oxford, and Gray's Inn, he had married in 1601 at Kinoulton church (Notts.), when aged 17, Gertrude Talbot, daughter of Henry Talbot, a younger son of George, 6th Earl of Shrewsbury, by his first wife. Henry Talbot was survived by two daughters, Gertrude and Mary. Mary married but died without issue, so all Henry Talbot's wealth was inherited by Gertrude and her husband Robert Pierrepont.

It would appear that the couple's early married life was spent at a Pierrepont residence in north Nottinghamshire, possibly Holbeck Woodhouse, as some of their six sons and three daughters were baptised at Mansfield. The principal Pierrepont residence was Holme Pierrepont, near Nottingham, where they would live following the death of Robert's father, Sir Henry Pierrepont, in 1615.

In 1627 Robert was created Viscount Newark and the following summer King Charles I made him Earl of Kingston-upon-Hull. On each occasion £4,000 changed hands. He held lands in Beighton (near Sheffield) where he was patron of the living. One wonders what exactly motivated the earl to purchase in 1639 the small manor of Oldcotes, but with six sons to provide for this may explain his interest. In March 1641 two gentlemen (with the initials H.L. and J.B.), servants of the 3rd Earl of Devonshire, arrived at Holme Pierrepont to submit to Lord Kingston a schedule detailing the lands to be included in the proposed sale of Oldcotes, which at twenty years' purchase, together with the woods and buildings, they valued at £5,023:[1]

> *The particulars that I gave to my Lord Kingston that his Lordship is to have in his purchase vizt.*

|  | £ | s. | d. |
| --- | --- | --- | --- |
| Henry Barker Smith medow | 004 | 00 | 00 |
| More the horse close | 002 | 13 | 04 |

---

[1] The following three documents are at Chatsworth and are printed here by kind permission of the Duke of Devonshire and the Chatsworth Settlement Trustees.

| | | | |
|---|---|---|---|
| Godfrey Tallence longe medow, Gillian holme close wood[1] | 013 | 13 | 04 |
| Mr Bereye brodfeild | 018 | 00 | 00 |
| more for the nue close | 002 | 10 | 00 |
| more for the longe close[2] neare Sutton park | 019 | 00 | 00 |
| more for the rough close[3] | 020 | 00 | 00 |
| Robert Watkinson barley close | 001 | 10 | 00 |
| William Kage the Ridinges | 007 | 00 | 00 |
| more for the stone delfe | 002 | 00 | 00 |
| more for white croftes & cow close wood | 024 | 06 | 08 |
| William Robertes the orchard | 000 | 18 | 00 |
| more for a pece near the orchard | 001 | 06 | 00 |
| more for a pingle called setinges | 000 | 13 | 04 |
| Roger Hill with others Shepard closes | 031 | 02 | 04 |
| Thomas March a tenement in Sutton parke | 007 | 10 | 00 |
| besides woodes growinge of that tenement part £10 | | | |
| | 156 | 03 | 00 |
| | | | |
| woodes growinge in oulcotes growndes of that is to be sold | 600 | 00 | 00 |
| All the buildinge uppon the landes | 1300 | 00 | 00 |
| The land at 20 years porchase cometh to | 3123 | 00 | 00 |
| | | | |
| | 5023 | 00 | 00 |

These are the particulers I gave my Lord.

This is the particuler, which was given in unto the Rt. Hon. Robert Earle of Kingston and these names of the closes abovesaid together with their interlyneinges abovesaid vizt. (or Cow close wood & Williamson medow and Ox close) and Carre and Staniforth sick Close are thought fitt by us to be used in the shedule for further explanation of the growndes which should passe. H.L. J.B.

A list was also drawn up of land at Oldcotes which was not to be included in

[1] 'or Cow Close wood & Williamson meadow' interlined here.

[2] 'and ox close' interlined.

[3] '& Carre & Staniforth sick close' interlined.

the sale to Kingston:[1]

|  | a. | r. | p. |
|---|---|---|---|
| Kirke Leyes conteynyng by survey about | 36 | 2 | 20 |
| Pearetreefeilds conteyning ut supra about | 35 | 1 | 10 |
| Breakes conteyning about | 09 | 3 | 20 |
| Haublins all of them conteyning about | 44 | 0 | 32 |
| Great and Litle Scoryes about | 05 | 0 | 36 |
| The Healdes about | 17 | 0 | 00 |
| Cartercrofts about | 16 | 0 | 10 |
| Well croft about | 01 | 0 | 30 |
| Twelve butts aboute | 02 | 0 | 20 |
| Boulsover nooke | 03 | 2 | 20 |
| Rye peece about | 03 | 2 | 20 |
| Sawell about | 05 | 0 | 00 |
| New close | 05 | 0 | 10 |
| Eight Leyes about | 02 | 1 | 30 |

Memorandum that all these parcells doe ly ypon the south side of the boundary of that part of oldcoats which is sold to the Earle of Kingston

All these by the Plott and booke of Survey are part of oldcoates but reserved to my Lord and not to passe in the conveyance to my Lord of Kingston with the rest of Oldcoates.

A comparison of William Senior's survey with that prepared for the Pierreponts in 1659 shows that the land to be retained by Devonshire lay on the south-eastern side of the estate, closest to Heath village. The earl may have reserved these lands because they were leased to his tenants in Heath village and were essential for their livelihood. In a letter dated 19 March 1641 Lord Kingston wrote to the Earl of Devonshire:

> My Lord,
> I am willed by thes Gentlemen your Lordship pleased to send unto me, to give your Lordship assurance that I have bargained with them, and agreed to ye cautions about this next Annunciation Rent and getting of coales[2] (they say) your Lordship prescribed, onely they would att first

---

[1] The schedule, which totals 186a. 2r. 18p., is endorsed in a contemporary hand: 'false as to number of acres'.

[2] i.e. 5s. per load of coal to be paid to Devonshire, other than for Kingston's use, or a fine of 5s. for every load not disclosed.

have had £5,000 of mee though the price I give being £200 Less (which godwilling your Lordship shall receive from mee in Easter Terme next and therein as early as I can) I should have held a vast & intollerable rate for so Litle, had I not a desire to Live, (for my short time) in Derbyshire, as your Lordship's faithfull servant) and a neighbour to ye ill-willer of your most honourable family the Lord Deincourt,[1] albeit perhaps I shall do so with his ill will. So ending with my humble thankfulnes to your Lordship (which shall have no conclusion but with my life) for your noble desire expressed to mee by your Lordship's said servants) that I should be your Lordship's chapman[2] before any other, I remain with my Prayers for the continuall happiness of you and yours.

My Lord, your Lordship's devotedly to serve you
Kingston

My Lord your servants mention some Irons unfixed in the chimneys, coffers & some wood already hewed for making bedsteds &c. I humbly referr to your Lordship's good pleasure myn having them (which I must accompt your bounty) or not having them, which I shall esteem ... [the rest is lost]

In May 1641 Christian, Dowager Countess of Devonshire, and her son the 2nd Earl of Devonshire conveyed to William Pierrepont, the second son of Robert Earl of Kingston, and two trustees what was described as the New House and the Old House in Oldcotes, parcel of the manor of Stainsby. A schedule attached to the deeds refers to 'two messuages one of them called the New House and the other called the Old House, situate and being in Oldcotes and all barns, stables, houses, buildings, appurtenances to them belonging ... and ... of the said passage and water course for the rest of the said messuage and do all other necessary for the carrying and conveying of the said water from the conduit to the springs of the said House called the New House'. A month later, Christian conveyed 'all that the manor of Oldcotes and Shepheards Closes with the appurtenances in the County of Derby' (and another manor in Lancashire) to her son William for £10,049 3s.[3]

William, the Earl of Kingston's second son, was aged 32 at the time of the

[1] Lord Deincourt, created 1st Earl of Scarsdale in 1645.
[2] i.e. a buyer or dealer.
[3] Chatsworth House, Hardwick Deeds, H/417/1–3.

purchase of Old-cotes, and was known to be residing at Thoresby (Notts.).[1] A man of great penetration and sound judgment, who retained the respect of both sides during the Civil War, he earned the appellation of 'Wise William' among his relations and friends. The continuation of the Pierrepont line as Earls of Kingston owes much to the descendants of this man. In 1644 William married, at Thoresby, Elizabeth Harris,

**Figure 10** Robert Pierrepont, 1st Earl of Kingston (1584–1643).

daughter and heir of Sir Thomas Harris of Tong Castle (Shropshire). This marriage produced five sons and three daughters. The second, third and fourth sons died unmarried, while the fifth, Gervase Pierrepont (1st Lord Pierrepont) of Tong Castle, although married, died without issue. William's eldest son Robert married, but died when he was only 34 (before his father). Nevertheless, he left three sons and a daughter. Henry, 2nd Earl of Kingston died leaving no surviving issue, so the title passed to Robert's sons, each in order of birth succeeding to their uncle Henry's title, and becoming the 3rd, 4th and 5th Earls of Kingston.

Their grandfather, 'Wise William', died in 1678 and was buried at Holme Pierrepont. He made his last will in 1677 in which he gave his London address

---

[1] The present house, the third, was built about 1870 near the site of a brick mansion which followed an earlier house by Talman, which was burnt down in 1745. Thoresby Park (200 acres) was formed in 1683 and is a fragment of Sherwood Forest.

as Lincoln's Inn Fields. This house and its contents he left to his eldest son's widow Elizabeth Pierrepont for the remainder of her life.


## George Pierrepont of Oldcotes

The sixth and youngest son of Robert, 1st Earl of Kingston, born in 1628, George Pierrepont was a schoolboy aged 15 when his father was killed. Although only 58 at the time of his death, the earl had made suitable provision for all his children. George's inheritance was to be the manor of Powick near Worcester, and the manor, lands and tenements in Middleton, Yorkshire, when he attained his majority, or on his marriage, whichever occurred first. However, following the death of their father, George Pierrepont's eldest brother Henry, then aged 36, became the 2nd Earl of Kingston, and in that same year (1643) Henry settled the manor of Oldcotes on his youngest brother George, on condition that George settled the manor of Powick on another brother, Gervase.

It would appear that *c.* 1648 when he was about 20, George married Mary Jones, the daughter of Isaac Jones, a Merchant Taylor of Broad Street, London. The family were of Shropshire origin, where they owned the manor of Sandford, and Isaac had also acquired considerable property in both that county and Surrey. Mary had a brother Samuel who in due course joined his father as a merchant. In 1647, a year before Mary's marriage, Samuel purchased the manor of Courteenhall, Northamptonshire, for £8,819 18s. 8d. He was a supporter of the Parliamentary cause.

George and Mary Pierrepont's first-born in 1650 was a son named Henry after her uncle, the 2nd Earl of Kingston; a second son Samuel, named after his mother's brother, was born the following year.

Isaac Jones died in 1652, when his son Samuel was High Sheriff of North-amptonshire, and Samuel inherited many estates. In 1656 he became MP for Shrewsbury, later becoming a supporter of Charles II, and was rewarded with a knighthood in 1660. As there were no children of either of his marriages, the Pierreponts' hopes of inheritance for their children must have been high, but later events were to cause problems.

A Parliamentary Survey of 1650 recorded for the parish of Beighton that the impropriate tithes, valued at £60, were held by George Pierrepont.[1]

Nothing is known of the amount of time his family spent at Oldcotes. George Pierrepont must have possessed qualities and accomplishment to fit him for entry into local society, yet his name never appeared on the list of gentry

[1] J.C. Cox, *Notes on the churches of Derbyshire* (1875–9), iv. 448.

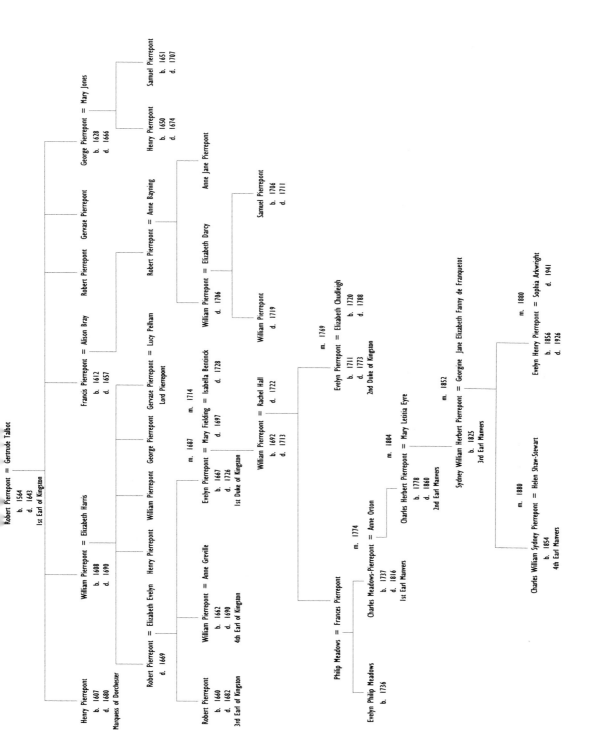

Fig. 11. The Descendants of Robert Pierrepont, 1st Earl of Kingston

43

accepting county office, which leads one to assume that the major portion of the year was spent in London. The author could find only one reference to George's presence in Derbyshire. This was in connection with the 1661 Act of Parliament to collect a free and voluntary present for King Charles II, who had returned to the throne in debt and without finances. On this occasion George Pierrepont subscribed £60, an amount only surpassed in Derbyshire by Sir John Curzon of Kedleston who gave £100.

According to Sir Samuel Degge, the Recorder of Derby, Mary Pierrepont died soon after the birth of Samuel. George made his will on 9 April 1663 when only 35 years of age. This may well have been precipitated by the early death of his wife. However, it proved fortuitous as three later George himself died.

*The will of George Pierrepont, dated 9 April 1663*[1]

In the name of God Amen. I George Pierrepont of Oldcotes in the county of Derby, Esquire, the nineth of April 1663, being in perfect health, praise be God do make and ordain this my last will and testament. [He then commends his soul into the hands of Almighty God and requests that his body be buried in the church of Holme Pierrepont amongst his ancestors]. First I give to my eldest son Henry Pierrepont, and the heirs male of his body all my estate in lands whatsoever in the County of Derby. Also I give unto him all my plate and jewels whatsoever. Next to my son Samuel Pierrepont and his heirs all my estate whatsoever which I have in the manor lands and tenements in Middleton in the County of York, which my late most honoured father, the Earl of Kingston, purchased of Sir Ferdinando Leigh and gave unto me. Also I give unto him all my estate in Sussex. Also I give him all my linen and household stuff belonging to my houses at Oldcotts and Morton. Provided that if my son Henry shall, within 5 Years after my decease, pay to my son Samuel the sum of £1,000, after such payment, the gift of household stuff to Samuel shall be void, and Henry shall enjoy it.

Likewise I give to the poor of the parish of Cuckney and Beigton £10 each. To the poor of the town of Calow, in the parish of Chesterfield, 20 nobles. To the poor in the parishes of Heath, Sutton Scarsdale and Babworth £5 each.

To each of my household servants at the time of my death £5 each, to be paid within six months of my departure.

I appoint my good and dear brother Mr William Pierrepont and my son

[1] Public Record Office, PROB 11/321, ff. 261r–v.

Samuel executors of this last will and testament, and entreat my said brother to take the burden and said paines upon him to assist my two sonnes in managing their estates, both for my two sonnes good in managing their estates and also for quieting of my estate. And I do give unto him £200, not as any reward but as a token of my true love and affection unto him.

The rest of my estate, my debts, funeral expenses without any pomp, and legacies being paid, I leave to my son Samuel, wishing him to be punctually careful in the payment of £100 yearly to Mr Richard Blake of the City of London, taylor, during his natural life, unto whom to such affect I have acknowledged a statute.

To my worthy well-beloved friend Mr Edmund Browne £30 yearly. To Hugh Wivell and Elizabeth his wife £50 yearly during their natural lives for their dear and good service to me. £80 yearly to Mrs Dorothy Wiseman, wife of Mr Richard Wiseman, chirurgeon, of the Old Bailey during her natural life, tied by statute. These annuities to be paid out of my manor, lands and tenements of Middleton, county of York.

In witness whereof I have set my had and seal the day and year above written.

(signed) George Pierrepont.


In the presence of Edmund Browne, Hugh Wivell, Elizabeth Wivell, Henry Whitworth, James Bradbury.


In all probability George Pierrepont made his will while in residence at 'Oldcotts', since it was witnessed by his 'well-loved friend Edmund Browne', who may have been his agent or attorney, and Mr and Mrs Wivell, who were in his employ, possibly as butler and housekeeper. No provision is made for his wife Mary, and so he was definitely a widower with two young sons. He stated that he was in perfect health and therefore had no reason to expect such an early demise. It would seem that during his lifetime he had purchased an estate in Sussex, as it was not part of his inheritance. That he had a house at nearby Morton is surprising. Although he states this house contained 'linen and household stuff' belonging to him, there is no inventory for this, and so perhaps it was tenanted. He requested an older brother William (his father's second son) to 'take the burden and paines' upon him for both his orphaned boys Henry and Samuel. This brother, known as 'William the Wise', was aged 58 when George died, and was in some ways a tragic figure, in that all his four younger brothers predeceased his, as did the first four of his five sons. A man of great possessions, with lands in the counties of Nottingham, Lincoln, York and Huntingdon, he was the ideal person to guide these boys.

George Pierrepont's early death on 1 July 1666 resulted in an inventory being taken of all his goods at 'Oldcotts' and in London.[1] No indication is given as to where he died, but we know that he was laid to rest with his ancestors at Holme Pierrepont on 7 July 1666 aged 38. The Plague had raged in London in the summer of 1665 and lingered on into 1666, but he could not have been one of its victims, or his body would not have been allowed to leave the city. Nor did he die as a result of the Great Fire of London, as that did not occur until after his death. The inventory of the contents of Oldcotes was taken on 23 August 1666, when for the first and only time in the mansion's history do we learn of the size and contents of this great house, which was eventually to disappear, leaving hardly a trace of its former glory.

*A true and perfect Inventory of all and singular the goods, chattels, and debts of the [late] George Pierrepont late of Oldcots in ye county of Darby Esq. deceased. Taken vallued and appraised the 23rd day of August 1666 by Richard Whitby of the Towne of Nottingham Uptholster, Thomas Stabing of Calow and William Smith of Heath as followeth, vizt.*

| | £ | s. | d. |
|---|---|---|---|
| *In the Hall* | | | |
| 2 Long Tables, 2 Long Formes, 2 shorter formes, 2 Short Tables with 2 Carpetts, 2 covered formes, 1 livery cupboard, a Great Iron Grate, 11 peeces of Tapestry hangings, an old Clock and a Glass Lanthorne | 20 | 15 | 0 |
| *In the Parlor* | | | |
| 1 Square table & Carpett, 2 Little tables and 2 carpetts, 1 Armed chaire, 12 black Stooles, .... Screene, a Grate Iron, 7 Cushions, 1 Long cushon, A tosting forke, a paire of Tables, ye hangings, 4 window Curtins and 2 Curting Rodds | 11 | 10 | 0 |

*In ye Little withdrawing Parlor*

1 Little Table, 2 Carpetts, 1 Little Iron grate, 11 Silke black Stooles, 4 peices of Tapestry hangings, window

<hr>

[1] PRO, PROB 4/10464. In the following transcript some punctuation has been supplied, the redundant 'Item' at the start of each entry has been omitted, and roman numerals have been converted to arabic.

Curtins and a Curtin rod.                                        22    0    0

### In the Chamber over ye withdrawing Parlor

1 bedstead,1 featherbed, 1 bolster, 2 pillows, 1 Silke twilt,
Curtins and Vallence, head Cloathe and teaster of red
plush, 1 little Table, a Carpett, an Armed Chaire, 2
black Stooles, and 2 other Stooles of red damaske, 1 old
Turkey Carpett, 4 peeces of Tapestry hangings, a Little
iron grate, 1 Close Stoole and pann, 2 window curtins
and 1 Rod                                                        22   10    0

### In the Nursery

2 bedsteads with old Curtins and vallence, 2 featherbeds
2 bolsters, 4 blancketts, 2 Coverings, one pillow, one Iron
Grate, 1 Broken Chaire, 2 old Stooles, a little table and
a paire of Tongnes.                                               6    0    0

### In the Nursery Clossett

1 Greate Presse, 1 Little Table and an old chaire              1   13    4

### In the Passage Roome

One Iron Grate, 2 presses, 1 Little Table, and one Buffet
forme                                                             6    0    0

### In the Chamber over the Kitching

1 Table, 1 Livery Cupboard, 2 Chaires, 2 Stooles, one
bedstead, one feather bed, 1 Matteres, 1 bolster, 2
pillows, 3 blancketts, 1 Counterpane, duble Vallence,
Curtins, head Cloath, and tester of Red Cloath with
greene Lace, 3 old Carpetts, 5 pieces of Tapestry,
a Close Stoole, and pann, one Iron grate, one fire
pann and tongnes.                                                22    0    0

### In the Closet belongong to the said room

Some glasses, one chaire, 2 window shutts, a Little

Table and a Greene Carpett.                          2    0    0

*In the Chamber over the Pastrey*

one bedstead, one feather bed, one bolster, 2 pillows,
4 blanketts, 1 Rugg, Curtins, vallence of Kiderminster
Stuffe, 1 Livery Cupbord, 2 Little Tables, 2 Chaires,
2 window Curtins and rods, 1 landiron, 2 froggs with
fire pann and tongs.                                 5   10    0

*In the Great Dining Chamber*

2 Armed chaires, 18 black Stooles and 3 Carpetts of Red
velvett, 1 Square Table, 2 Side Tables, 5 Spanish Tables,
2 Persian Carpetts, a picture with a gilt frame, one iron
Grate and brass andirons, and 9 pieces of Tapestry   113   0    0

*In the Gallery*

40 Gilt Leather black Stooles, 14 Candlesticks, 1 Great
Looking Glass, a billiard Table, ye gilt Leather hangings,
an Iron Grate, and 2 andirons of Brass               34   10    0

*In the Blew Star Chamber*

1 bed stead, 1 feather bed, one bolster, 2 pillows, 1 Blew
Sarsnett twilt, 1 white twilt, one blankett, duble curtin
and duble vallance                                   16    0    0

*In the Same Roome*

One Table, 1 Carpett, 12 Black Stooles and 2 other
Stooles   of branched crimson velvet, 1 Grate of iron,
1 fire pann and tonges                                    16   00

*In the Best Chamber*

1 bedstead, 1 feather bed, 1 twilt, one blankett, duble
Curtins and duble vallence, 1 silke twilt, 2 Armed
chaires, 6 Stooles, 2 Little tables, 2 dressing Tables,
2 folding Screenes, 3 foot Carpetts, 5 peices of tapestry,

48

a Great  Looking Glass, 3 window Curtins and Rodds,
a  Close Stoole and pann, an Iron grate, fire Shovell
and tongs                                                                          32     0     0

*In the Little roome belonging to ye Best Chamber*

1 feather bed, 2 bolsters, 1 bedstead, Curtins, Coounter-
pane and vallance, 1 old peece of tapestry, 2 peeces
of verders, an Iron Grate, 2 Andirons, a little table,
a Yallow table cloth, 2 Stooles, 1 Chaire and a Close
Stoole frame                                                                      3     10     0

*In the Chamber over ye last roome*

1 bedsted, 1 feather bed, 1 bolster, Curtins, vallens,
tester and head peice and Counter pane, 2 blancketts,
one old Side Table, 1 Carpett, a Livery Cupboard and
carpett, 1 Chaire, and 3 little Stooles                                3     10     0

*In the inner wardwrobe*

1 bedsted, 1 halfheaded bedstead, 2 feather beds,
2 bolsters, with some old bedcloathes, a Greene Carpett,
1 press, 2 andirons, and an old horyen Chaire                   5     0     0

*In the outer wardrobe*

1 bedstead, 1 feather bed, 1 bolster, 2 blancketts, 1 rugg,
Curtins and vallance, a Cradle, an old bolster with other
houslements                                                                      3     0     0

*In the uppermost chamber under the Tirrit*

1 bedsted, 1 feather bed, 1 bolster, duble vallance,
5 blancketts, 1 Setle, and 1 Side Table                             2     10     0

*In ye Red Velvet Chamber*

1 bedstead, 1 feather bed, 2 blancketts, 1 bolster,
1 Counterpane, duble vallence and curtins, one
Matteres, 1 Side Table, with a Carpet, 2 chaires,

| | | | |
|---|---|---|---|
| 1 Iron Grate, a window curtin and rod, one black Stoole, 6 peeces of Tapestry. | 13 | 0 | 0 |

### In the Greene Damask Chamber

| | | | |
|---|---|---|---|
| 1 Bedstead, 1 feather bed, 1 bolster, 1 pillow, 1 Mattereste, 1 white twilt, 4 blanketts, duble vallence, curtins, ... cloath Counterpane, tester, 1 Carpett, 1 Armed chaire, 2 black Stooles all of greene damaske, 2 Side Tables, 1 Carpett, 1 iron Grate, 7 peices of Tapestry, 2 window Curtins and a Curtin Rod | 23 | 0 | 0 |

### In the High Red Chamber

| | | | |
|---|---|---|---|
| 1 bedstead, 1 feather bed, 1 bolster, 1 matteres, 2 blanketts, Counterpane, duble vallence, Curtins, head cloath and tester, one foot carpett, one other Carpett, 2 Armed chaires, 4 Stooles, one window Curtine and rod, one half headed bedstead, 1 feather bed, 1 bolster, 1 blankett, 1 Rugg, 1 Matteres, 1 grate, with the hangings about the Seeling | 15 | 0 | 0 |

### In the Tawney Chamber

| | | | |
|---|---|---|---|
| 1 bedstead, 1 bolster, 1 featherbed, duble vallence, Curtins, head peice, tester & Counterpane, 1 blankett, 1 old Rug, 1 Side table, 1 Carpet, 2 Armed Chaires, 1 Stoole, 1 Iron Grate, 6 pieces of Tapestry | 13 | 0 | 0 |

### In the Upper Staire head Chamber

| | | | |
|---|---|---|---|
| 1 bedstead, Curtins and vallence, 1 feather bed, 1 bolster, 1 Coverlet, 2 blanketts and 1 Table | 2 | 15 | 0 |

### In ye Little Chamber next ye Lining chamber, or butlers roome

| | | | |
|---|---|---|---|
| 1 bedstead, 1 feather bed, 1 bolster, with Some old bed cloathes | 1 | 3 | 4 |

*In the Cookes Chamber*

| | | | |
|---|---|---|---|
| 1 bedstead, 1 bolster, 1 feather bed & some old bed cloathes | 1 | 13 | 4 |

*In the wet Larder*

| | | | |
|---|---|---|---|
| 1 planke, 1 kimnell | | 10 | 0 |

*In the Pastry*

| | | | |
|---|---|---|---|
| 2 dressers, 4 pedistales, 1 Kimnell, 1 churne & a little cubbert | 1 | 6 | 8 |

*In the Inner pantry*

| | | | |
|---|---|---|---|
| One Plancke table, 2 pedistales, a little cupboard, 1 Stoole, 1 forme, 1 Side table, 2 black Jacks and other hushlements | 1 | 0 | 0 |

*In the outer Pantery*

| | | | |
|---|---|---|---|
| 2 planke Tables & pedistalls, 1 other Planke with Shelves, 1 forme, 2 Sutes and formes, 3 dozen of Candles, 5 buttery basketts & other hushlements | 2 | 2 | 0 |

*In the Sellers*

| | | | |
|---|---|---|---|
| 13 Thralls, 6 dozen of Bottles & other hushlements | 1 | 0 | 0 |

*In the New Kitching*

| | | | |
|---|---|---|---|
| 2 dressers, 1 Planck, 2 Little formes & other hushlements | | 10 | 0 |

*In the New Porters Lodge*

| | | | |
|---|---|---|---|
| 1 flock bed, 2 Ticks for bolsters, a Little handiron & firepan and other hushlements | | 10 | 0 |

*In the Old house kitching*

2 chaf beds, 2 blankets, 1 Coverlet, 2 brewing Tubbs,

| | | | |
|---|--:|--:|--:|
| 2 Little Tables and other hushlements | 1 | 10 | 0 |

*In the Old Hall and boulting house*

| | | | |
|---|--:|--:|--:|
| Some old Hogheads, an Old Still, 1 kneading Trough, a moulding Table with other hushlements | | 13 | 4 |

*In the old house Parlour*

| | | | |
|---|--:|--:|--:|
| 1 bedstead, 1 halfe headed bedstead, 3 feather beds, 6 bolsters, 3 blanketts, and 4 Coverletts, 2 Side Tables & an Iron grate | 7 | 0 | 0 |

*In the old house Dayrey*

| | | | |
|---|--:|--:|--:|
| 4 Planckes & other hushlements | | 10 | 0 |

*In the old house Buttery*

| | | | |
|---|--:|--:|--:|
| 3 hogsheads, 1 barrell, 2 thralls, one Plank & other hushlements | | 6 | 8 |

*In the old house Dineing Roome*

| | | | |
|---|--:|--:|--:|
| 2 Settles, 2 Tables, 1 Side Table, 2 Leather Chaires, 3 Stooles, 2 Armed chaires and an Iron Grate | 1 | 0 | 0 |

*In the old house South Chamber*

| | | | |
|---|--:|--:|--:|
| one bedstead | | 6 | 8 |

*In the Dayry Chamber*

| | | | |
|---|--:|--:|--:|
| 2 feather beds, 1 bolster, 4 Pillowes, 1 bedstead, vallence, Curtins, tester, and head peece, 2 Livery Cupboards, A Looking glass, 1 Chaire, 2 Stooles, a Close Stoole and pann | 6 | 0 | 0 |

*In the Middle Chamber in ye old house*

1 bedstead, 2 feather bedds, 1 bolster, curtins & vallance,

| | | | |
|---|---|---|---|
| a little Table, one Stoole & a little grate of Iron | 5 | 0 | 0 |

*In the old house Passage*

| | | | |
|---|---|---|---|
| 1 bedstead, 1 feather bed, 1 bolster, Some old bed cloathes, 4 Sadles, a Little ... & other hushlements. | 3 | 13 | 4 |

*In the Chamber Over the Ovens*

| | | | |
|---|---|---|---|
| 1 feather bed, 1 bolster, a Little table, a half headed bedstead, with other hushlements | 1 | 3 | 4 |
| The bowles in the Clossett | 1 | 10 | 0 |

*In the New halls Kitchin*

| | | | |
|---|---|---|---|
| 3 Sid plancks, 1 Settle, a great dresser, 8 Sptts, 2 Clevers, 1 Jack, 2 racks, 1 Stay iron & 1 plate Iron, 2 frying pans, 2 planks in ye passage, 2 fire Shovels, a paire of tongs, pot hookes, 1 beefefork, 1 dripping panne, ... doz. of Trenchers, 2 warming panns with Basketts, Kitts & other hushlements, 4 brass Candlesticks, 1 brass morter, 3 chafeing dishes, 2 brass Scumers, 532 pounds of Pewter, 175 pounds of pan brass & 42 pounds of Pott brass | 42 | 12 | 0 |

*Plate*

| | | | |
|---|---|---|---|
| 596 ounces of Silver plate at 5s. 2d. per ounce | 153 | 19 | 2 |

*In the Brewhouse*

| | | | |
|---|---|---|---|
| 3 tubbs, 1 Cooler lined with Lead, a brewing Lead, a Lead Cesterne, Some garthes with other hushlements | 20 | 0 | 0 |

*In the yard*

| | | | |
|---|---|---|---|
| 3 old Cowes | 3 | 0 | 0 |
| the Coles gotten | 5 | 0 | 0 |

*In the Lining Room*

6 paire of Holland sheets & 1 odd one, 16 paire of
Linning sheets & 1 odd one, 3 damask Table clothes,
3 paire of Harding sheets, 1 Large Holland diaper table
cloath, 3 Fustian diaper table Cloathes, 4 fine Flaxen
Large table cloths, 7 table clothes for the Hall, 34 Large
diaper napkins, 13 indifferent table Napkins, 11 damask
napkins, 6 of them fine ones, 24 damask napkins, 1
damaske Table cloth, 25 flaxen Napkins, 52 flaxen
Napkins indifferent, 6 paire of Holland Pillowbeeres,
5 paire of linning pillowberes, 3 Flaxen Towells,
6 dresser cloathes & Seaven rubbing cloathes,
1 dimothy old sheet and rubbing cloath                    15    9    8

5 paire of Servants Sheets, 2 paire of lining Sheets,
3 paire of Holland Sheets, two Scotch cloth cupboard
clothes, 4 paire of Holland Pillowberes, 5 linning
Pillowberes, 24 fine linning Napkins, 24 Ordinary
Napkkins, 4 Ordinary Towells, 2 walletts, 6 rubbers      12    2    8

Fowre Spinning wheeles, Lumber & hushlements             2    12    9

The pump Cesterne of Lead, a Lead weight, a Table
under the great Staires & a Bell uppon the leades         6    0    0

*In the old Porters Lodg*

1 old bedstead, 2 flockbeds & other hushlements               15    0

*Goods of the deceased att Mr Wisemans house att London
appraised by Ralph Gale & John Wilson as foll. vizt.*

1 Silver tankerd, 6 Spoones, 2 porringers, 3 salts and
1 Long Spoone, a silver tobaco box weighing 77 ounces
att 4s. 11d. ye ounce                                    18    18    7
A pocket Clock                                            6    0    0
A gold tobaco Stopper                                     2    2    6
A Specticle case and specticles                                3    6
an old Sute & coate & shoos & Stockins                    1    10   0
a peece of old damask                                          14    0

| | | | |
|---|---|---|---|
| part of a Tobacco Role 15 lb weight | 3 | 7 | 6 |
| 2 Perriwigs | 2 | 0 | 0 |
| a hatt | | 18 | 0 |
| a Sword & belt and Staff | | 14 | 0 |
| a mourning gowne & wastcoate | 1 | 0 | 0 |
| 7 old holland Sheets and 2 paire and one odd sheete | 1 | 14 | 0 |
| 2 old Cupboard cloathes | | 4 | 0 |
| 11 old Billowberes & 3 old Towells | | 7 | 6 |
| 1 whole Shirt, 4 Calico half Shirts all old | | 16 | 6 |
| 9 old Napkins | | 4 | 0 |
| 7 Pockett handkerfchers & 8 old bands full of holes & Cuffes | | 5 | 0 |
| an old Bible | | 3 | 0 |
| a Cupboard and close Stoole & old Skreene att | 2 | 5 | 0 |
| an old Coach Covered with mourning & harnes For six horses appraised by John Rotherham & Cordwell Slater att | 7 | 0 | 0 |
| 6 black Coach horses appraised by Henry Waters and Edward Tompson att | 50 | 0 | 0 |
| | | | |
| Summa | 806 | 17 | 11 |

George Pierrepont died on 1 July 1666, but the inventory was not taken until 23 August, almost two months later, which may account for the 'unoccupied' feeling one has regarding this property. No provisions are listed, no clothing and no animals, apart from three cows. It is as though all perishable goods and all living creatures had been whisked away, and the fully furnished mansion left awaiting an occupant.

The three appraisers of this detailed inventory were all men of integrity. Richard Whitby, upholsterer of Nottingham, would be the ideal person to value the furniture, and indeed some of it may have been made by him. Thomas Stabing (perhaps this should be Stubbing) was a member of a well-to-do Calow family, and possibly a tenant of Pierrepont's, while William Smith of Heath tenanted a large area of land at Heath and worked a number of small coal pits.

The inventory lists the contents of 47 rooms. In the principal rooms and chambers the walls were covered with tapestries; in all there were 56 pieces and one set of 'gilt and leather hangings' in the gallery. The 1601 inventory of the Great Chamber at Hardwick Hall listed six pieces of painted and gilded leather hangings. Perhaps William, 1st Earl of Devonshire brought these to Oldcotes.

The hangings would have helped to warm the rooms and the screens shielded the occupants from draughts. Back stools were the most popular form of seat. Although the inventory definitely uses the word 'black' in connection with the numerous stools, the author believes the appraiser meant back. The heavy voluminous skirts of the ladies and the padded suits of the gentlemen made sitting in a relaxed posture difficult. The stools were fairly high and had short backs to them, thus the ladies were able to raise their skirts and perch on the stools.

The gallery, which contained no less than 40 'gilt leather black stools', was long and narrow, the walls hung with leather gilt wall hangings. It contained a great looking glass and a billiard table. The gallery was used for promenading in inclement weather and as a games room. It had no pictures or portraits, indeed there was only one gilt framed picture in the whole house and that was in the dining chamber.

The great dining chamber contained two armed chairs for the master and mistress and 18 black stools for guests and family. The room was warmed by a coal fire and nine pieces of tapestry covering the walls. The five Spanish (mahogany?) tables were probably identical so that they could be placed end-to-end together to form a big table. Two side tables to accommodate dishes and a square table were covered with red velvet carpets. Such table coverings were called carpets. The floors were covered with either rushes or rush matting. The bedchamber floors were bare with possibly a small foot carpet near the bed.

The best chamber appears to be one of the most comfortable chambers in the house. The four-poster feather bed was complete with bedding and double-curtains to keep out the draughts. The room was well furnished with two small tables and two dressing tables. The fireplace, complete with shovel and tongs, meant that the room could have a coal fire. There were three foot carpets to warm the floor, the walls were covered with tapestries, and the three windows had curtains to exclude the draughts. This room had a great looking glass, a close stool and pan (night commode). A little room (possibly windowless) led off the best chamber. This too was comfortably furnished and was for the use of a lady's maid or gentleman's manservant.

Other bedchambers are named after significant features. The Blue Star Chamber probably had a blue ceiling decorated with stars or the ceiling of the four-poster bed was blue and decorated with stars. The Red Velvet Chamber, the Greene Damask Chamber, the Tawney Chamber all refer to the curtains, valances etc. belonging to the four-poster beds.

As in all great houses of this period the main entrance opened into the hall. This was at all time a busy thoroughfare, with servants toing and froing. It was often two storeys high. The hall contained long tables and forms at which the servants would sit for their meals, and a great iron grate where a fire burnt night and day. There was a livery cupboard where food was kept for refreshment for callers. The only clock in the whole house was here, and the glass lanthorne would burn throughout the night. There were eleven tapestry hangings which indicates the size of this hall.

The inventory refers to the 'room over the ovens'. Ovens were never described in inventories as they were just stone-lined wall cavities used for baking bread, cakes and pies. They bore no resemblance to modern or even Victorian ovens. The fire was kindled inside them, the stones absorbing the heat, and when the fire died down the ashes were swept out and bread etc. pushed into the oven, which was sealed during baking. The heat from such ovens warmed the room above.

The totals of each item of furniture etc. is revealing: *Tables:* in all 48. Types: long, short, square, little, side, Spanish and dressing. *Stools:* in all 131. Types: black 46, black silk 11, gilt and black leather 40, red damask 2, broached red velvet 2, black and green damask 2, and 28 others. *Tapestries:* in all 56, and one set of gilt leather hangings. *Chairs:* armed chairs 13, chairs 15, buffet 1. *Forms or Planks (for tables):* 15. *Settles* 4. *Dressers* 5. *Cupboards* 2. *Presses* 4. *Carpets for Tables:* in all 26. Turkey 1, green 2, red velvet 3, Persian 2. *Foot Carpets* 3. *Rugs* 4. *Cushions* 8. *Livery Cupboards* 6. *Folding Screens* 3. *Window Curtains* 17 pairs. *Bedsteads* 30 and 4 half-headed. *Beds:* 30 feather, 3 flock, 2 chaff, 5 mattresses; 9 beds had curtain hangings and vallances, head cloth and testers, and 9 had curtains and vallances. *Linen:* 20 pairs of pillow cases, 35 pairs of sheets, 19 tablecloths, 183 napkins, 27 towels, 13 rubbing cloths, 26 bolsters, 13 pillows, 39 blankets, coverings and counterpanes 20. *Close stools and pans* 5. *One picture* in a gilt frame. *Candlesticks:* 14 and 4 Brass. *One old clock. Looking glasses:* 2 great and 1 other. *One Cradle. Spinning Wheels* 2. *Saddles* 4. 532 lb. of pewter (plates and dishes etc.), 175 lb. of pan brass, 42 lb. of pot brass. Total value £42 12s. 596 lb. of silver Plate at 5s. 2d. per lb., £153 19s. 2d. *Kitchen and dairy* contents included 3 jacks, 1 kneading trough, a moulding table, 2 frying pans, pot hooks, 1 beef fork, 1 dripping pan, 3 chafing dishes, 2 brass scummers, 5 buttery baskets. *Brewing Etc.* 2 tubs, 1 barrel, 4 hogsheads (large cask for liquor), 1 old still, 6 doz. bottles, 3 tubs, 1 brewing lead, 3 doz. candles, 2 warming pans (to air a bed), a brass mortar. The pump cistern of lead, a lead weight, a table under the great stairs and a bell upon the Leads (on the flat roof).

In the New Hall kitchen the roasting spits, gridiron, gallows and racks are all missing. Had they been removed before the inventory?

The goods belonging Mr Wiseman at the Old Bailey (this 'very private man') hold the secret to an intriguing puzzle. Certain items of clothing, two perriwigs, a mourning gown and waistcoat, the old bands, cuffs, spectacles and Bible, one associates with the profession of lawyer or clergyman. George Pierrepont never attended either Oxford or Cambridge or the Inns of Court, as did his father and older brothers. Bearing in mind that he was only 15 when his father was killed and his brother William was twenty years his senior, it may be that William undertook to supervise George's further education. Although William had been admitted to Lincoln's Inn when he was 20, and had an address in Lincoln's Inn Fields, he never became a barrister, but had an interesting political career.

George might have pursued a legal career outside the Inns of Court as a member of an Inn of Chancery. There were ten of these which performed an educational role similar to that of the Inns of Court, but at a lower level. Their members did not have the right to represent clients in court, and performed more routine legal tasks. George may have been an attorney and a member of one of these smaller Inns. Unfortunately, no record of attorneys go back that far. This assumption, if correct, would account for him occupying a room or lodgings at Mr Wiseman's house in the Old Bailey, where he had the comfort of his own possessions. A puzzling point relating to this inventory is the comparison between his affluent possessions and his poor clothing and linen, especially when we learn that he left his tailor an annuity of £100! Presumably his gown covered his old clothing. Perhaps his mourning coach and black horses denoted he was still in mourning for his wife.

## The unsolved puzzle

The inventory of 1666 makes it possible to understand something of the internal layout of Oldcotes, which, as the almost contemporary estate map shows, was by this date a three-storey house with the most important rooms on the first floor. It is impossible to be certain whether the house originally had only two storeys plus turrets, as Smythson's drawing shows and Senior's representation appears to indicate, to which a third storey was added sometime before 1659, or whether Bess modified Smythson's design to give the house three main floors from the start. Similarly, if a two-storey house was later enlarged, it is impossible to say whether this was done before or after 1641, when the estate changed hands, although it is far more likely that a new owner would make the alterations.

As with all Smythson's buildings, the ground floor at Oldcotes appears to have been divided symmetrically, with hall and parlours to one side, and kitchen and associated rooms such as pantry, larder and pastry on the other. The high first floor had the principal rooms: the Great Dining Chamber and the Best Chamber, the Gallery (with billiard table), and the main bedrooms, namely the Blue Star Chamber and the Best Chamber. The second floor had other furnished bedrooms named after their dominant decorative material or colour: the Red Velvet Chamber, the Green Damask Chamber, the High Red Chamber and the Tawney Chamber. Another chamber was described as situated beneath the turret. Separate chambers for the butler and cook were mentioned, but on which floor they were situated is unclear. The building also had cellars. The inventory lists possessions in the hall, parlour, dining room chamber, kitchen, dairy and buttery of the Old House. On the 1659 plan there are several buildings in front of the mansion to the south-east. This spot is still occupied by a building of coursed rubble sandstone, of irregular plan with gable ends on all four sides, infilled openings and a low floor level, all suggesting a structure of some age with parts added on. It seems quite possible that this building is a survivor from the 'Old House', i.e. the house that preceded Bess's mansion of the 1590s.

## Henry Pierrepont of Oldcotes

Henry, the elder son of George Pierrepont, succeeded at sixteen years of age to all the Pierrepont lands in Derbyshire, which included the manor of Oldcotes, part of Calow and lands and tenements in Beighton, as well as the advowson of Beighton. There is no evidence of 'William the Wise' fulfilling his late brother George's request in respect of the care of his two orphaned sons, making them competent to assume overall supervision of their estates when they achieved their respective majorities. Henry's early education remains a mystery. He matriculated at St Edmund Hall, Oxford, when eighteen, but there is no record of his obtaining a degree. As a minor, it would seem that his maternal uncle, Sir Samuel Jones, assumed certain responsibilities, for when William Jessop was inducted to the living of Beighton, Sir Samuel was named as patron.[1] Henry's name appears in the Hearth Tax assessment for 1670, and we learn that in respect of Oldcotes he was responsible for the astonishing number of 48 hearths.[2] The collectors did not enter the premises but reckoned the number of chimneys from outside.

The 1666 inventory lists possessions in 27 rooms of the main house, and in four others described as closets and wardrobes; cellars and kitchens are also mentioned, but how many rooms these represent is not stated. Twelve rooms are listed as being in the Old House, which appears to have had only two storeys. There were also new and old porters' lodges and a separate brewhouse. In total twenty rooms had iron grates or equipment that implies the presenceof a fireplace. Doubtless other fireplaces must have existed unmentioned in some

---

[1] J.C. Cox, *Notes on the Churches of Derbyshire* (1875–9), iv. 448.

[2] *Derbyshire Heath Tax Assessments, 1662–70* (ed. D.G. Edwards) (Derbyshire Record Society, 7, 1982), pp. xlix, 175.

other rooms, as in the kitchens and brewhouse. The total, however, is difficult to match with the Hearth Tax, as 48 hearths would make Oldcotes the fifth largest house in Derbyshire. This figure must surely include other buildings such as cottages and the adjoining farmstead.

Henry definitely resided at Oldcotes, as is proved by his appearance as a witness in deeds. Sir Simon Degge asserts that Henry 'entered into his possession and married', but the name of his bride is not divulged. Sadly Henry died in early manhood and only enjoyed his inheritance for a mere eight years. He was obviously a sick man when he made his will in 1674. It is brief and his only brother Samuel is his sole beneficiary. No friends or servants were remembered, nor did he stipulate where he wished to be buried, leaving it to Samuel his brother to make this decision. He was buried at Holme Pierrepont where the register records: 'Henry Pyerepont Esqr. was buried December the twenty and one 1674'. He was only 24 years old.

*The will of Henry Pierrepont, dated 20 October 1674*[1]

In the name of God Amen. I Henry Pierrepont of Oldcotes in the County of Derby Esquire, being weake of body but of sound and perfect memory and understanding. Praise be rendered to Almighty God for the same considering the frailty and instability of human condition do make and ordain this my last will and testament in manner and form following. First and principally I commend my soule into the hands of Almighty God my creator in Confidence and full assurance of the salvation of the same in and through the meritts and mediation of my Saviour Jesus Christ. My body I commend to the earth from whence it came, to be decently buried at the discretion of my Executor hereafter named. As for my worldly estate both real and personal I give and devise to my Brother Samuel Pierrepont (after my just debts paid and funerall charges expended). And do hereby make him the said Samuel executor of this my last will and testament. Revoking all other and former will and wills by me heretofore made. In witness whereof I the said Henry Pierrepont have hereunto sett my hand and seale the Twentieth day of October in the Six and Twentieth year of the reigne of our soveraigne lord King Charles the second over his Realms of England. Anno Domini 1674.

Hen: Pierepont

---

[1] PRO, PROB 11/348, f. 348.

Signed, sealed and published in the presence of George Milward, Francis Bainbridge, Henry Whitworth.

All three witnesses were men in his employ.

Henry's will and subsequent death gave rise to certain legal problems, and litigation must have proved expensive for his brother Samuel, for among Degge's papers were found questions and answers posed on behalf of Samuel to Degge shortly before Henry's death, as the date of the reply coincided with the date of Henry's burial, 21 December 1674. The basic facts were stated thus: 'Henry the elder son and heir came of age about 3 years ago and entered into the premises and married ... The said Henry dyed in the beginning of this instant December 1674 and upon his death the said Samuel Pierrepont entered into the premises ...'. The question then posed to counsel was: 'Whether the Relict [i.e. widow] of Henry Pierrepont can recover dower in the premises?', and the answer was: 'The widow of Henry Pierrepont without doubt hath right of dower, her husband being tenant in tayle, and the issue which he had or might have had by her being inheritable'. Thus, although Henry had made no provision in his will for his wife, some provision would have to be made as she had a right to dower. This would certainly reduce Samuel's inheritance. Who the lady was remains a mystery, but the fact that Henry died without issue left the way clear for Samuel to inherit and occupy Oldcotes.

The next question shows how Samuel was endeavouring to break the entail. It asked: 'Whether the said Mr Samuel Pierrepont tenant in taile cannot dock and cut off the intayle and which way it might be done. The said Mr Samuel Pierrepont and his heirs males of his body being the last in Remainder'. The answer: 'I conceive a fine without any Recovery will barr this estate tayle and all but the lease for years which I suppose is to be attended on the reversion and ought to be surrendered there being no daughter or daughters to expect the benefit'.

## Samuel Pierrepont of Oldcotes

Nothing is known of Samuel's early life or of his education. Prior to his brother's death he may well have resided at the Morton house, which would account for his acquaintance with the 'cock-fighters' of nearby Higham. Following his brother's death he definitely lived at Oldcotes, and it seems unlikely that he ever maintained any other residence. He was 23 when he inherited Henry's Derbyshire lands in addition to his own, thus making him a very wealthy man. He does not appear to have taken interest in county affairs, although in 1702 he was appointed a deputy lieutenant for Derbyshire. The first

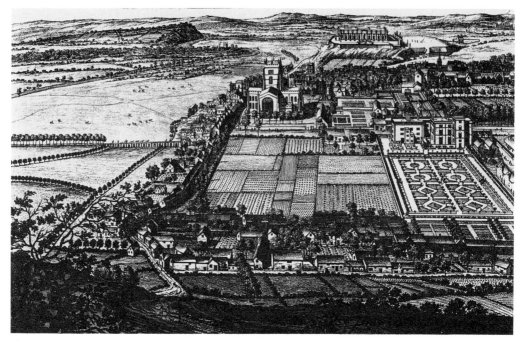

**Figure 12** Nottingham from the east *c.* 1707, with Pierrepont House and its elaborate formal gardens on the right.

we hear of him was in 1687 when Leonard Wheatcroft, the parish clerk of Ashover, wrote the following:[1]

*An Epigram on his Honour's Birthday*
*Samuel Pierrepont of Oulecoates in Derbyshire upon May 29 1687*

Then let's with him rejoice with joy and mirth
That we have such a peer to treat the earth,
Who is the age (as Freak this day me told)
No more nor less—but 34 years old.

He was in fact 36. Freak, a cottager on the Mansfield road, Heath, may have been in Samuel's employ and was doubtless well rewarded for obtaining this ditty.

By 1690 Samuel had sold the patronage of the living of Morton to his cousin Francis Pierrepont of Pierrepont House, Nottingham, but retained the patronage

---

[1] C.E. Lugard (ed.), *The inns and outs of Ashover* (1923).

62

of Beighton.[1] A letter sent by Robert, Earl of Scarsdale to Thomas Coke of Melbourne, dated November 1701, evidently refers to Samuel: 'This morning I sent to my neighbour Pierrepont who promises me his interest in you and to take care that all his votes shall attend'. This refers to a forthcoming parliamentary election. Jonathan Adlington, a Chesterfield bailiff between 1760 and 1780, recorded in his diary[2] an account of a great cock fight which took place at the beginning of the century at Calow Green between:

*His Honour Pierrepont of Oldcotes*
*and the Coal Miners of Higham*

1.   One twenty third of June, next to Midsummer Day
      Our blackguards[3] went to Calow, 3 shakebags[4] to play
      Against His honour Pierrepont there;
      At the White Horse[5] we did appear (both cocks and men)
      We took money plenty, ne'er a pocket empty was there to be found
      Likewise a gallant piper,
      Played before us to the ground.

2.   But when this grand appearance
      Was made on Calow Green
      His Honour he declared
      The like was never seen,
      To see the sons of Hector then,
      Durst appear before such gentlemen,
      Three shakebags for to play,
      O then we boldly entered, and our money ventured
      And so freely did it lay.
      Little white son of Old Blinkard
      Won the first shakebag that day.

3.   Oh! then we got our dinners
      And we thanked 'em for their Gold,

---

[1] Cox, *Derbyshire churches*.

[2] Chesterfield Local Studies Library, Metcalfe Collection.

[3] Coalminers.

[4] Cock fights.

[5] The White Horse disappeared from Calow some three centuries ago and a stackyard owned by a Mr Lowe occupied its site. When an inn it was kept at the time by a Mary Stones.

We was become great winners
So plain we did behold
Then falling to our work again
We shewed 'em Benjamin's Dun to ease their pain
By force of Arms like great Mars he then died,
And their Champion plund'red
And soon had laid him low
Little Dun had soon assured us
Which way more Gold must go.

4.    Now we have slain two monsters
The third we're resolved to try,
Soon we had subdued him,
For our Black Grey did him beguile.
For soon as these two cocks did meet
Cheetham's Black Grey his heels did wet
Which made the blood to foam,
Then Redferne fell a roaring
When he saw him goring,
Which made the bagpipes blow,
We was then all well assured
Which way our Gold must go.

5.    Now we have slain three monsters,
Lie reeking in their bleeding gore,
Sought by the best of Gamsters
And ne'er able to strike once more.
But now we've got your Guineas
We'll make the White horse Whinney
And drink liquors store,
Hoping your Noble Highness
Will fight us Blackguards no more.

6.    Now we will return to Higham
Towards our native place,
Filling our sides with liquor,
And the piper shall grace us,
Oh! then at Stretton we bartered,
And our Musick Treated,
If you'll be pleased to know,
And when we came to Higham,

64

Many favours we did bestow.

FINIS.

This doggerel was written by the piper named Enoch Elliott of Woolley who accompanied the Higham miners to Calow. Pierrepont sought the match, and Sir Jonathan Jenkinson of Walton Hall handled the cocks for him. W.E. Godfrey believed 'His Honour Pierrepont' referred to George Pierrepont,[1] but this cannot be so, as he died in 1666, while Jenkinson (who handled the cocks) did not die until *c*. 1740.

In 1671 Sir Samuel Jones of Courteenhall, Samuel Pierrepont's maternal uncle, set out the proposed disposition of his estate in Northamptonshire, Oxfordshire, Shropshire, Denbighshire and Surrey. As he had no direct heirs he bequeathed all his properties to his nephew and namesake Samuel Pierrepont, second son of his late sister Mary Pierrepont, on condition that he change his surname to Jones. But a year later, a codicil dated 16 September 1672 was added, partly because of the death of one of his nephews, 'But most of all by the idle and unprofitable life of my indiscrete nephew Samuel Pierrepont'. So incensed was he at this unspecified misbehaviour that Pierrepont was deleted from the will. The estates were then left to another nephew Samuel Wake for his life, and his sons after him, on condition that he changed his name from Wake to Jones.

The young Samuel Wake Jones, his great-nephew, and his heirs were 'to avoid the sinns of Drunkennesse and Debauchery now so much in fashion and betake themselves during their younger years to the study of the Law and that they be industrious to imitate the examples of the best men and be deterred from the commitment of evil by the consequences which they observe doe attend the committers of it'.[2]

Sir Samuel Jones died in 1672. A man who laid great store by the value of a good education, a different side of his character is seen in his philanthropic activities. A charming reminder of him is the school which he provided in his will. Built in 1680 it stands to the west of the present house. The pupils were to be taught English, Latin, Greek, writing and casting accounts, Samuel Pierrepont's 'indiscretions' were obviously well known to his uncle, and Samuel must have felt keen disappointment and regret at the loss of such a large inheritance which would have made him an exceedingly rich gentleman, but his arrogance and self-esteem were such that he in no way changed his ways.

It would seem that during the ownership of Oldcotes by Samuel's late

[1] Chesterfield Local Studies Library, Godfrey Notebooks.
[2] Peter Gordon, *The Wakes of Northamptonshire* (1992), pp. 68–9.

**Figure 13** Monument to Sir Samuel Jones and his wife Mary in Courteenhall church (Northants.), 1672.

brother Henry, Edmund Browne had been succeeded by Francis Bainbridge as estate agent. He is a witness to Henry's will. In 1688 Francis Bainbridge revised and completed the 1659 plan of Old-cotes, 'after ye ponds and park were made and replenished in ye yeare 1688'. Presumably Samuel Pierrepont, anxious to complete with neighbouring nobility, and in consultation with Bainbridge, created the ponds and the deer park. The plan as revised shows the park enclosed within a fence running along Shire Lane on the west, the boundary with Sutton parish on the north, and the brook forming the boundary of the Oldcotes estate (as it was after the sale of 1641) on the south. On the east, the fence runs almost due north-south through fields to the east of the mansion.

Today a public footpath, which begins near Heath church and ends near Park Corner Cottage at Sutton Scarsdale, follows this eastern park boundary almost exactly between the two streams forming the southern and northern boundaries of the park.

Within the park, the 1659 map shows three small ponds to the south of the house, fed by a stream which flows into the brook forming the southern bound-ary of the estate, which has itself beem dammed near the point where it joins the Doe Lea to form a fourth, rather larger pond. The park was said to contain 162 acres, so that it occupied somewhat less than half the land at Oldcotes (excluding Shepherds Closes) purchased by the Pierreponts in 1641.

The 1659 plan, as revised in 1688, also shows a layout of formal grounds on all four sides of the main house, whereas Senior simply marks a 'Court' to the north of the house and a corresponding (unnamed) area to the south. It is not entirely clear whether this more elaborate arrangement was already in existence in 1659 or whether it was another of the improvements carried out between then and 1688. The plan shows the court to the north of the house as a walled garden, divided into two by a central path running north from the house, gated

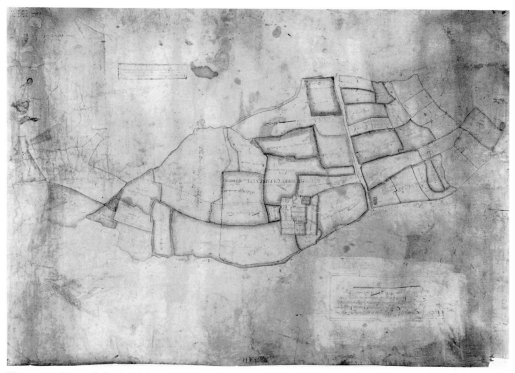

**Figure 14** Map of the lordship of Oldcotes belonging to Samuel Pierrepont 1659 (revised 1688).

at each end. In the middle of each portion of garden some kind of garden building is shown, too indistinctly drawn to make out its exact form or function. To the west of the house was a paddock, created from a close named Barn Croft in 1609; to the east there was an orchard and an 'Old Bowling Green' enclosed from part of Cow Close. In front of the house on its main (southern) side there was another area of garden, surrounded by walls and divided into three by two paths running north-south, with trees shown in the two outer compartments. Rather oddly, what is presumably the more important path, since it runs from the gate in the garden wall to the south, ends not at a doorway in the centre of the house (where there is in fact no entrance shown) but to a door located between the second and third bays from the left-hand end of the main front. The other path simply runs from the garden wall to the house, with neither a gate at one end nor a door at the other. As in the case of the extra storey, there is thus a discrepancy between the Smythson drawing (which shows a front elevation arranged symmetrically either side of a central doorway) and the estate map (which is clearly attempting to show the house realistically), where the only entrance is some way off-centre.

At the eastern end of the front garden wall the map shows the gabled building that is almost certainly the 'Old House' of the inventory of 1666. To the south again was a larger enclosed area named 'The Great Garden', and beyond that what appears to be a farmyard, with an extensive, irregular range of buildings along its eastern and southern sides, laid out to form two separate quadrangular groups. The south-western corner of this area was occupied by a separate half-acre enclosure, presumably for stock that needed to be kept close to the farm.

From the time they had purchased Oldcotes, the Pierreponts had always occupied a special pew in the old Heath church, situated at Lound, because Oldcotes manor lay within the parish of Heath. In 1706 this church was newly seated, the pulpit rebuilt, 'to which the vicar, the Rev. Edward Revell has contributed £10'. And 'to

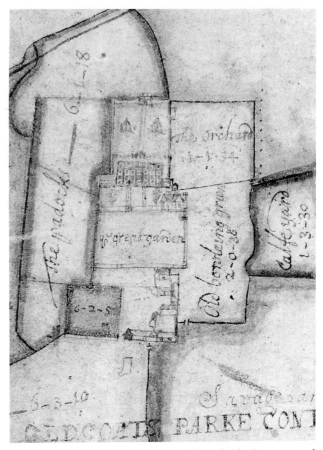

Figure 15 Detail from Browne and Bainbridge's survey of Oldcotes of 1659–88 showing the mansion and grounds.

which a good velvet cushion with tassels, pulpit cloth, a cloth for the Reading Desk, and a decent good carpet for the Altar of purple coloured cloth, and a carpet with a deep silk fringe [were given]. The noble benefactor is ye Hon. Samuel Pierrepont of Oldcotes Esq., and upon the pulpit cloth is embroidered in gold S.P.'. This was all noted by Bassano, the Derby herald, in his notes on his visit to Heath in 1710.

By this date Samuel had been dead for three years. One wonders if there had been some disagreement between Samuel and the vicar of Heath, since Samuel was not buried in his own parish but in the neighbouring parish of Sutton. In the Heath register his death is recorded thus: '8 Sept. 1707 obit Samuel Pierrepont de Oldcotes infra parochiam de Heath, Armiger, Nobilis eodem die depositum fuit in ecclesia parochiae de Sutton-in-le-Dale 1707'. Samuel must have been on very friendly terms with his neighbour Robert, 3rd Earl of Scarsdale, patron of the living, whose permission would be required. The Sutton register reads: 'Samuel Pierrepont Esq. of Old-Coates in the parish of Heath was buried September 8th 1707'. His resting place within the altar rails is marked by a large black marble slab bearing the initials S.P. Also a large ornamental monument, complete with a bust and heraldic arms of the deceased was erected on the East wall of the sanctuary, inscribed:

Near unto this place lies the body of
Samuel Pierrepont, the
second son of the Honorable George Pierrepont Esq.
the sixth son of ye right
honorable
Robert, Earl of Kingston
The said Samuel was never married
and died ye sixth day
of September
one thousand seven hundred and seven
in the fifty sixth year
of his age.

Incidentally this ponderous monument proved expensive for the parish as the east window had to be moved out of alignment to accommodate it and a large buttress built outside to support its weight.

If the bust on his memorial is a true likeness—and there is every reason to believe that it is—then one can be sure that Samuel dressed in the height of fashion. In all probability he was a great spender and gambler like his friend and neighbour Robert, Earl of Scarsdale, for they were roughly of the same age, although Samuel did not enjoy such an exalted status as the earl. Nevertheless, Samuel was very conscious of his position in life, as the wording of his will demonstrates: 'To be buried according to my Quality and Degree'. His death took place when the Act of Parliament for burying in woollen was in force, but in accordance with his 'Quality and Degree' he was buried in linen and his executors paid the necessary fine. His was the only corpse buried at Sutton which did not conform to the Act.

Following Samuel's demise a survey of Oldcotes was made in 1707, which shows that the house was still surrounded by a walled park, as at Sutton, although the acreages vary somewhat from those of 1688:[1]

---

[1] Beth Hampson, 'History of Heath' (Unpublished typesript, *c.* 1950; copy in the present author's possession).

| | a. | r. | p. |
|---|---|---|---|
| Within the Park Wall inclusive of the mansion | 107 | 0 | 13 |
| Demesne without the Park Wall used and belonging to the mansion House | 159 | 1 | 00 |
| New House Land | 83 | 0 | 01 |
| William Hancock's Land | 43 | 3 | 19 |
| Total | 453 | 1 | 13 |

This survey shows that the Shepherds Closes portion of the estate west of Shire Lane was regarded as a separate holding (of 83 acres) and has been renamed New House Land. This presumably implies that the farm now known as High House, which stands within this area, had been built by 1707, although evidently not long before this date.

Samuel Pierrepont's will is dated 1 August 1707.[1] He bequeathes his soul into the hands of Almighty God and asks that his body be interred in Sutton church according to 'his Quality and Degree'. He appoints John Statham of Tideswell and his faithful servant Edward Nevill gent. his executors, to whom he leaves all his manors, lordships, lands, tithes, tenements and premises in trust for various uses, so that by sale, mortgage or lease they may raise money to pay his debts, legacies and funeral expenses. Also they are to keep all sums of money that from time to time become due to recompense themselves for the trouble, cost and charges incurred in executing the trust. Afterwards, Statham and Nevill are to 'stand seized of the aforesaid premises' to the use of Samuel's godson, Samuel Pierrepont, the younger son of his cousin William Pierrepont, late of Nottingham Esq., for the term of his life, and after his death to his first son, with remainder to other sons in tail male in order of seniority. The remaindermen were his godson's elder brother, William Pierrepont; Gervase, Baron Pierrepont; Lord Newark, son of Evelyn, Marquess of Dorchester; Evelyn, Marquess of Dorchester; and the right heirs of Samuel Pierrepont.

Samuel's also made bequests to his servant John Cowsell (£400 for his care and good service); to Mrs Ann Hill (possibly his housekeeper), who was to be allowed 'peaceably and quietly to take and carry away all her goods and chattels in or about Oldcoates House without the molestation of my executors or of any person whatsoever'; to all his domestic servants living with him at the time of his decease and for six years before (except Jeremiah Yates), one half year's wages more than is due to them; to all his tenants (except John Germaine, Robert Green, John Newbold, Thomas Ingman and George White) one half year's rent abated; to the poor of Sutton and Duckmanton £5; to the poor of

[1] PRO, PROB 11/495, ff. 264v–265v.

70

Beighton £5; to the poor of Calow £5; to the poor of Heath 50s.; to the poor of Ardwick-on-Dearne (Yorks.) £5; and to John Statham and Edward Nevill 50 guineas each in token for undertaking the trusteeship. He also empowered his executors to claim their costs from the estate and to charge the estate with any legal expenses in defending the trust. 'And if any such action shall be brought or prosecuted by any of the persons the Legatees in this will I doe from thenceforth vacate and destroy such Legacy and doe only give to such person One Shilling in lieu of such legacy.'

Finally, Samuel noted that he and his his 'Ancestors have usually made a yearly allowance towards the better maintenance of the Minister of Beighton for the time being' and he empowered his executors 'to continue, alter, or take away the said pension allowance as they in their discretions shall see meete.'

**Figure 16** The monument to Samuel Pierrepont in Sutton Scarsdale church.

The will was witnessed by Thomas Slater, Thomas Smith and Gervase Balguy. It was proved in London by Thomas Statham and Edward Nevill on 17 November 1707. The original will is endorsed with a receipt dated 20 February 1709, signed by Nevill, who returned it on 12 April 1718. This may indicate that there was some opposition to its provisions. That some problems did arise is clear from the advice of counsel (signed H. (or S.) Turner and unfortunately undated) preserved among the papers of Adam Wolley, the Matlock attorney and antiquary:[1]

*S.P.'s WILL*

Q.1: What power have the Executors by this will and what part the personal estate? *Answer:* I conceive no part of the personal estate is in any ways disposed of by his Hon. Mr Pierrepont's will therefore all his personal estate falls to his Executors.

---

[1] British Library, Add.MS 6668, f. 137.

Q.2: When does the Trust determine? *Answer:* When all the debts and funeral expenses and all charges are defrayed and paid then in execution of the Trust, then and not before, the Trust determines. And then they stand seized to the use of Samuel Pierrepont as in the will.

Q.3. One of the Executors has a lease of part of the estate—does the devisee drown the lease or extinguish the rest?[1] *Answer:* The estate in fee is devised to the Executors in Trust and I conceive if the Trustee that hath this lease assigned it over to any other person in trust for him before he takes upon him this trust his term may be performed.

Q.4: Does the advowson of a Church pass by this will to the Executors? *Answer:* I conceive the advowson of the Church passes to the legatees in trust as well as all other lands by virtue of the words tenements and hereditaments.

## The favoured godson: Master Samuel Pierrepont

William and Elizabeth Pierrepont of Pierrepont House, Nottingham, already had a son (William) when their second child, also a boy, was born. They asked William's bachelor cousin, Samuel Pierrepont of Oldcotes, to be the baby's godfather. One can imagine how proud and honoured the middle-aged Samuel felt as he stood godfather to this little boy who was to bear his name. The baptism took place at the nearby parish church of St Mary's, Nottingham, and is recorded in the register thus: '8th March 1705/6 Samuel, son of William Pierrepont, esquire, and Elizabeth his wife'. As a second son the child's inheritance would not be great, but his godfather could change that by breaking the entail, and Samuel had every intention of leaving his entire inheritance to his namesake. This intention was further strengthened when the boy's father William Pierrepont died six months later and his burial is recorded in Holme Pierrepont register: '5th/6th[2] September 1706 William Pierrepont of Notting-ham, esquire'.

Very little is known about 'young Sam' except that he was the great-grandson of Francis Pierrepont, third son of the 1st Earl of Kingston, and that his father was MP for Nottingham from 1695 until his death in 1706. Destined to die in childhood, he is referred to briefly in 1708. Sir William Dawes, Bishop of

---

[1] This was Edward Nevill, who has a lease of New House and land.

[2] The figure has been altered.

Chester, was journeying through his diocese, accompanied, among others, by his deputy registrar who kept a diary of the day-to-day visits. The group entered Derbyshire on 18 August. One member of the party for part of the way was 'Mr Statham of Tideswell, an Attorney and Trustee for young Mr Pierrepont'. Riding through Chesterfield they arrived at Mr Nevill's near Oldcoats where 'about 12 o'clock, we walk down to Oldcoats, observe the great but inconvenient model and contrivances, dine after with Mr Nevill. The dinner was substantial, the beer good and old, the wine decayed'. Invited, they walk the half mile to the Earl of Scarsdale's at Sutton, where they were well received and hospitably entertained for two days. On 20 August they were indisposed from the strong beer at Mr Nevill's and the indisposition continued the following day till relieved by a nap in Sutton church where the bishop preached in the forenoon, and 'following another exquisite dinner, prayers in Church, after we returned to the long corks'.[1]

Nevill was an executor of Samuel Pierrepont's will and also a trustee for young Samuel. It would seem that as agent he was acting as the caretaker of Oldcotes, which appears to have been unoccupied at the time, following Samuel Pierrepont's death. Young Samuel's next and final appearance is in the Holme Pierrepont register: '15th Dec. 1711, Samuel, son of William Pierrepont, late of Nottingham, esquire, and Elizabeth his wife, was buried in the vault'. He was aged 5 years 10 months.

Matters were not as simple as the executors had been led to believe, because Samuel Pierrepont had inherited estates in tail male, in which they had to remain. Samuel had endeavoured to break the entail by leaving his inheritance in the first place to his godson and, if this line failed, has clearly dictated the order of inheritance. Among Adam Wolley's papers are some writings of Sir Simon Degge, Attorney and Recorder of Derby, which contain some enlightening information concerning Samuel's will.

Presumably Degge's services had been engaged by the trustees Statham and Nevill, and Degge in turn had applied to John Chesshyre of the Inner Temple to whom he submitted a case for opinion:

> The Testator intended by the will annexed to make John Statham and Edward Nevill Trustees and Guardians for his godson and not to be accountable until he comes of age, and because there were *great threatenings by the heir* at law he gave his Executors 50 Guineas a piece to encourage 'em, but always intended them the personal estate which was of small value and which the Executors have disposed on and have done

---

[1] J.E. Heath, 'A bishop's summer journey into the East Midlands in 1708', *Derbyshire Miscellany*, ix (2) (1980), pp. 43–5.

several minor bequests which the Testator privately intimated to 'em he was desirous to have 'em doe.

*Question:* When does the Court determine, (the heir being but 2 years old) and what method will be safest for the Trustees to act and make him allowances for maintenance? *Answer:* I conceive that after the Trustees have by the meaning of the will raysed sufficient money as will together with the personal estate pay and discharge the debts and legacies, and also the charges of the will and the execution of the Trust, the estate in law will be executed and vested in the devisees still subjected to such charge as shall arise and be fit to be reimbursed within the intent of the will. And since the Executors are not appointed to do ward of this infant devisee I do see that after sufficient money is raysed for payment of debts and legacies reimbursing the charges of the execution of the Trust that the Executors are concerned in the taking the profits of the estate or allowing maintenance to ye devisee.

Other queries were raised and answered, but to quote them would in no way further our story of Oldcotes. Litigation, always an expensive business, must have dragged on for some years and proved a positive field-day for the lawyers. Suffice to draw the reader's attention to the two additions to the will following the grant of probate. Clearly the case was still active as late as 1719. Chesshyre's answers are dated from the Inner Temple, 18 November 1707.

## 'Man proposes but God disposes'

Samuel Pierrepont of Oldcotes had died secure in the belief that in his will he had accounted for every possible eventuality. However, the grim reaper played havoc with his carefully selected order of inheritance. In the event of the death of his godson and namesake, the young Samuel Pierrepont of Nottingham, the next in succession was to be the child's older brother William, but the Holme Pierrepont burial register records: '23rd May 1719, William Pierrepont, esquire, son of Mrs Pierrepont, widow, and relict of William Pierrepont, of Nottingham, esquire'. He died unmarried and without issue. The third in line had predeceased this William. He was the cousin of Samuel of Oldcotes, namely Gervase Pierrepont, created Baron Pierrepont of Ardglass (an Irish title) in 1703 and Baron Pierrepont of Hanslape (in the English peerage) in 1714, who died in 1715 without issue.

The fourth in line was William, Lord Newark, son of Evelyn, Marquess of Dorchester. William, styled Earl of Kingston from 1706, married young, but died aged 20 of smallpox in 1713, and in the lifetime of his father Lord Dorchester, who in 1715 was created Duke of Kingston. Newark left a son and heir Evelyn, born in 1711, who was only two when his father died, and thus became the heir of his grandfather. When the Duke of Kingston died in 1726, he was duly succeeded by his grandson, then aged 17, who became the 2nd Duke of Kingston and also proved to be the right heir to Oldcotes manor and all other manors and properties of the late Samuel Pierrepont of Oldcotes.

It is obvious that the whole question of rightful inheritance of Oldcotes manor must have been a nightmare for the two executors, Thomas Statham and Edward Nevill.

## New House or New Hall

It has already been noted that a survey of 1707 describes the land previously known as Shepherds Closes as 'New House Land'. A quarter of a mile south-west of Oldcotes and on the opposite side of Shire Lane stands this 'New House', situated on an eminence and with farm buildings set around a courtyard immediately to the rear. Built of coursed rubble sandstone with ashlar sandstone dressings, it has a tile roof with stone-coped gables. The house faces south, the main front having five bays with a parapet and pilasters at the angles. This handsome façade makes it most unlike an ordinary farm house. New House evidently dates from the beginning of the eighteenth century or the end of the seventeenth, since it is not shown on either the original estate map of 1659 or the revisions of 1688. The first recorded occupant was Edward Nevill, Samuel Pierrepont's faithful servant and one of his executors, but it remains unclear when exactly he moved in. His name appears for several years from 1713 as a witness to the passing of parish accounts and from the highways surveyors' accounts for that year comes the information that he was paid for stone for the repair of Heath roads:

|  | £ | s. | d. |
|---|---|---|---|
| Pd Mr Nevill for 113½ lods of stone at 6d. per lod | 2 | 16 | 9 |
| Pd Mr Nevill for 66 lods at 2d. per lod |  | 11 | 6 |
| Pd Mr Nevill for leading stone 17 days at 3s. 4d. | 2 | 0 | 0 |
| Pd Mr Nevill for leading stone 9 days | 1 | 10 | 0 |

Another interesting entry for 1713 is:

| | £ | s. | d. |
|---|---|---|---|
| Pd John Mosley and his partners for 66 loads of stone from Oldcoats at 4d. per load | 1 | 2 | 0 |

75

Was this stone from a quarry, or do these entries signify that Oldcotes was being demolished around this date and the rubble being used as roadstone? Perhaps more interesting is the possibility that the parapet and pilasters at New House were removed from Oldcotes when it was taken down and used by the agent to the Pierrepont estate to embellish a new house of his own.

Whatever was happening at Oldcotes at this time, it is obvious Nevill was involved. In 1715 he was paid 13s. 4d. for four days work and in 1717 we learn 'there is wanting 4 lays[1] from Mr Nevill, 10s.' Heath parish register contain this entry: 'Ann the wife of Mr Edward Nevill of New house was buried the 19th Dec. 1722'. The same register three months later records that 'Mary, the supposed Daughter of Mr Nevill and Rebekah Stephenson was privately Baptised in ye house (not being well) the 28th day of March 1723'. In 1724 the constable's accounts include:

| | |
|---|---|
| For fetching a warend[2] for Mr Nevill | 1s. |
| For going to ye Justis with Mr Nevill | 1s. |
| To ye Justis Clark | 1s. |

This is the last entry concerning him in the parish accounts, but the following is recorded in the Heath churchwardens' accounts:[3]

*May 8th, 1724*

Whereas I Edward Neville of New Hall in the Parish of Heath have formerly been at the Expence of Erecting a Loft at the West end of the Parish Church of Heath.

I do hereby give and grant, for ever, the said Seats to the Farmer Sonns of the said parish at my Decease, upon Condition that they Write upon the Seats the Gift of Edward Neville. Witnesse my hand.

*Edw. Neville*

Witnesses: Joseph Allwood, Samuel Houldsworth, Churchwardens, John Whildon, James Whildon, Richard Atkinson, Frances Houldsworth.

Nevill must have left the district shortly after this date, as he was not buried with his wife, and it is another fifty or so years before we can name the next tenant of High House.

---

[1] i.e. money due to the poor rate.

[2] i.e. warrant.

[3] Derbyshire Record Office, D1610 A/PW 1.

# 'The Right Heir': Evelyn Pierrepont, 2nd Duke of Kingston, 1711-73

Directly descended from William the Wise, the successful second son of the 1st Earl of Kingston, who purchased Oldcotes manor, Evelyn was vastly wealthy, having inherited Holme Pierrepont and Thoresby in Nottinghamshire, with its 1,200-acre park enclosed from Sherwood Forest by his great-uncle the 4th earl. Oldcotes manor must have seemed a small and minor inheritance, in which he had little interest except as a source of revenue. He had a sister, Lady Frances Pierrepont, who married Philip Medows of Brook Street, Hanover Square, London, of whom we shall hear more later.

The duke's sister and her husband Philip Medows had two sons. The elder, Evelyn Philip Medows, named after his uncle the duke—with the hope of inheritance—was born in 1736, and his brother Charles Medows was born the following year. Some time later the duke disinherited his eldest nephew Evelyn because of his cruelty to his mother and sister, and his attempts to quit active service in the late war highly offended the Duke. He found it impossible to continue on friendly terms with him. The duke thereafter favoured the younger nephew Charles. As a young man Evelyn enjoyed life to the full, showing no inclination to marry until in middle life he formed a permanent attachment for a lady-in-waiting at the Court named Elizabeth Chudleigh, who was secretly married to a naval officer named Hervey. She continued for some years as the duke's mistress, until, believing that she had obtained an annulment of her secret marriage, she married him in 1769, thus becoming the Duchess of Kingston.

When the duke died in 1773 at the age of 62, leaving no male issue, his titles became extinct. His will revealed he had left

> the annual sum of £4,000 to my wife, the Duchess of Kingston ... And my said wife shall be permitted during her widowhood to receive and take yearly rents and profits of all the manors and lands as shall grow due during her widowhood but in case my said wife shall determine her widowhood during her life[1] then I shall give and devise the same to Charles Medows, second son of Philip Medows. Also I bequeath to my said wife Elizabeth, Duchess of Kingston, all my furniture, pictures, plate, jewels, and all other of my effects and personal estate for her own proper use absolutely for evermore.

---

[1] i.e. re-marry.

Thus Oldcotes now became the property of the Dowager Duchess of Kingston, and she is recorded as supporting the farmers of Heath in a dispute with their vicar regarding the payment of tithe.[1] Meanwhile the storm clouds were gathering around the duchess, who, once her husband was dead, had more enemies than friends, the most vicious being the late duke's eldest nephew Evelyn Medows, who refused to believe that she was ever legally divorced from Hervey, and brought a case of bigamy against her. The duchess elected to be tried by her peers in the House of Lords, who found her guilty; she claimed peeress's privilege and thereby escaped punishment for felony. The remainder of her life was spent in travelling on the Continent. She died on 20 August 1785 in Paris, and her remains were brought home to England for burial at Holme Pierrepont.[2]

**Figure 17** Elizabeth Dowager Duchess of Kingston at her trial in the House of Lords in 1776.

Evelyn Medows gained nothing from his attempt to disprove his uncle's will, which brought on him only financial loss. However, magnanimous even in defeat, the duchess did not forget the man who had sought to bring about her downfall. Not only did she defray the ruinous costs of his case, because she felt he had reason to dispute his uncle's will, thinking her to be Kingston's mistress and not his wife, she allowed him £600 a year, and in her will bequeathed him £15,000 and all her gold and silver plate.

On her death, Charles Medows inherited the Kingston estates (including Owlcotes, as it was now generally known) under a settlement by the duke, and took the name of Pierrepont by Royal Licence. In 1796 he was created Viscount Newark and became Earl Manvers in 1806. When he died in 1816 he was succeeded by his son Charles Herbert, 2nd Earl Manvers (born in 1778), who

[1] Hampson, 'History of Heath'.

[2] For this colourful figure see Lewis Melville (ed.), *Trial of the Duchess of Kingston* (1927); C.E. Pearce, *The amazing duchess* (1931); and D. Leslie, *The incredible duchess. The life and times of Elizabeth Chudleigh* (1974).

died in 1860, leaving two sons, Sidney William Herbert Pierrepont, who became the 3rd Earl Manvers, and Evelyn Henry Pierrepont (born in 1856) who in 1880 married Sophia, the youngest sister of William Arkwright of Sutton Hall.

In 1910 William Arkwright purchased Owlcotes and High House (which bordered on his Sutton Estate) from the 3rd Earl Manvers, who reserved the minerals under the estate, which at the time were let to various local colliery companies. The two farms remained part of the Sutton Estate until this was broken up by sale in 1919, when Owlcotes was sold to G.J. Welch for £4,000 and High House to T.A. Lambe for £2,200.[1] In 1931 Owlcotes came on the market again, when the vendor was Allen & Orr Ltd.[2]

## Time's Ungentle Hand: Oldcotes Manor after 1707

The 'right heir', Evelyn, 2nd Duke of Kingston, did not require Oldcotes as a residence for he had other homes including Holme Pierrepont, Thoresby, and Pierrepont House, Nottingham, besides at least one London residence. His only interest lay in the income to be derived from the estate. Just as nearby Sutton House was enlarged and heightened to three storeys in the seventeenth century, a similar sequence of events may have happened at Oldcotes. Possibly heightened in the mid seventeenth century, the building was probably considered old-fashioned by the early or mid eighteenth century. As we have seen, a visitor to Oldcotes in 1708 described it in words which suggest an imposing and cumbersome building whose design was by then out-of-date. However, instead of being remodelled, the Duke of Kingston took a more expedient course.

Built and completed by the same men responsible for Hardwick Hall, there is no reason to believe that Oldcotes's structure was any less sound, although some repairs may have been required due to neglect by the Pierreponts arising from the dispute over the succession and ownership. Nevertheless, it was demolished—it did not become a ruin—and it is an established fact that Samuel Pierrepont was the last occupier. We have already mentioned the distinct possibility that some of the decoration from Oldcotes was used by Edward Nevill for his 'New House' a short distance away, and that he sold rubble to the surveyors to repair the parish roads. It may also be that stone from Oldcotes was used to rebuild the existing farmhouse, now known as Owlcotes, which still stands on the site. Facing east, the main elevation of this house consists of four

[1] Priced sale catalogue in author's possession.
[2] Sale catalogue in author's possession.

**Figure 18** Holme Pierrepont Hall, near Nottingham, engraved for Robert Thoroton's *History of Nottinghamshire* (1676).

bays, with a deeply recessed centre bay. The house is built of rubble sandstone, with sandstone dressings, and has a stone-slate and tile roof with stone gable and stacks. In its present form it appears to date from the early eighteenth century. On the other hand, part of the house—the south gable facing the garden with an immense outside chimney flue—is much older.

The only structure at Owlcotes today that appears to belong to Bess's mansion is an alcove, built into the garden wall, which was obviously a garden seat. Elsewhere on the farm, a curvilinear stone has been set on a boundary wall. This stone, similar to shaped examples used on the main frontage at Hardwick to emphasise the letters ES (Elizabeth Shrewsbury) must once have decorated a frontage at Oldcotes.

Although the mansion itself has entirely disappeared, it is possible to locate its position quite precisely by comparing the layout of the gardens shown on the estate map of 1659 with first edition of the large-scale Ordnance Survey map, surveyed in 1875, when several of the boundary walls survived. From this it is clear that the existing farmhouse occupies the same site as the gabled building which stood in the south-east corner of the inner front garden of Bess's mansion in 1659 and which appears to be the Old Hall mentioned in the inventory of

1666, i.e. the Savages' manor house that preceed the New Hall at Owlcotes. Even without a detailed survey, it is obvious that parts of this house are older than the eighteenth century. Second, buildings are shown in 1875 to the south of the farmhouse in almost exactly the same position, and with the same layout, as the buildings shown in 1659 to the south of the 'Great Garden'. Indeed, there are still buildings there today.

Given the ease with which walls and buildings shown in 1659 can be related to what is shown on the earliest modern large-scale map and to what can be found at Owlcotes today, it is simple enough to locate the position of those features which have disappeared since 1659—the mansion, the front garden to the south, the terrace running round the other sides of the

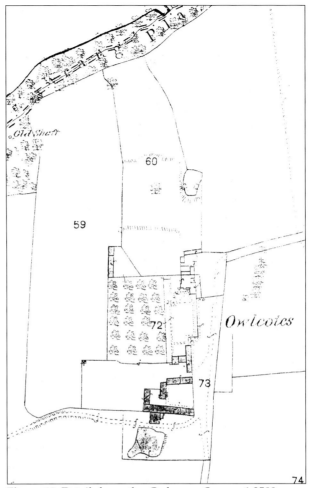

**Figure 19** Detail from the Ordnance Survey 1:2500 map, surveyed in 1875 (Derbys. XXVI.13), showing Owlcotes.

house, and the walled back garden to the north. This exercise in fact reveals that two apparently meaningless features on the Ordnance Survey map—the two parallel lengths of embankment shown running west–east to the north of the farmstead—represent the edge of the terrace behind the mansion and the end of the back garden. The closeness with which the layout shown in 1659 can be related to a modern map is quite striking and makes it possible to locate on the ground, probably to within an accuracy of a couple of metres, the position of both Bess of Hardwick's mansion at Oldcotes and the gardens that existed to the north and south of the house in the mid seventeenth century.

During the summer of 1997 an archaeological survey of Oldcotes was conducted by Richard Sheppard and colleagues from the Trent and Peak Arch-

**Figure 20** The alcove in the garden wall at Old-cotes, sketched in 1897.

aeological Trust, based at Nottingham University.[1] This located the site of the mansion to the north-west of the present farmhouse, on a flattish area bounded on its northern and north-eastern side by a break of slope, as shown by the Ordnance Survey in 1875. A geophysical survey was undertaken here, covering an area of 40 by 50 metres. Although the results were generally disappointing, a clear distinction could be seen to either side of an west–east fence-line that today divides the area. North of this line, the area is used for pasture for cattle; to the south there is a paddock used for housing stock or poultry. While a few isolated high readings were recorded in the former area, the paddock gave consistently high readings, suggesting the presence of much stone below the top soil. Although these differences may be due to differential treatment in clearance of the soil or debris, it may equally indicate that the building lay in the southern part of the area studied. The high readings may be caused by the rubble debris left when the building was demolished.

The survey suggested that the mansion may have been about 40–45 metres long and up to 20 metres deep. Robert Smythson built both near-rectangular houses and linear ones, the latter with a length-to-width ratio of about 2:1. Hardwick Hall, for instance, is 58 metres long and 28 metres deep. Perhaps a closer parallel to Oldcotes is Doddington Hall (Lincs.), which was built by Smythson at the same time, between 1593 and 1600. This is smaller than Hardwick and, like Oldcotes, is flat-roofed, without gables, and built with a minimal amount of ashlar. Inside it has a ground-floor hall, a great chamber on the first floor and a long gallery.

[1] The assistance of Richard Sheppard of the trust with the discussion that follows is gratefully acknowledged.

## Oldcotes and High House Farms

From the mid eighteenth century the lands belonging to the manor of Oldcotes became two separate farms lying either side of Shire Lane, the road from Heath Common to Sutton Scarsdale. The house once known as New House, New Hall or New House Farm now became High House, due to its excellent position on an eminence. Following Edward Nevill's disappearance from Heath after 1724, according to the parish register, New House was farmed by James Brailsford, whose son William was baptised at Heath on 8 August 1727, no mother's name being given. Two boys and two girls were baptised on later dates as the children of James and Mary Brailsford. It would seem that the next tenant was Joseph Hurt, for there is a record of him farming High House in 1777 and he may well have been there some time before this date. His first appearance in the parish records was in 1767 and again in 1769 when he was elected overseer of the poor for Heath. He also sold large quantities of stone to the parish for the repair of the roads. Later parish records state that in 1777 he had sheep on Heath Common and a Joseph Armstrong lived there and worked for him.[1]

Meanwhile Thomas Greaves senior, who had been farming Oldcotes with the help of his son Thomas Greaves junior, moved across the road to High House in 1786. Records show that the elder Thomas was connected with the Owlcotes Colliery which was sunk between 1799 and 1802 at Muster Brook on the boundary of the Hunloke estate in Williamthorpe. Mention is made of the carriage of coals from here to Thoresby. Extant is the following letter to Lord Newark's agent:[2]

*High House, April 1800*

Sir, I wrote to you some time since to Inform you that we was in great wants of some Wood to make a Gin we have 2 pitts open for getting Coal but they are too Deep to be drawn by hand. Therefore if you cannot Conveniently come over at present please to give me or some Other person Orders to set out a few Trees to be getting forward for the above Use they have been filling here more than a fortnight and seems to go Very well and I'm afraid if Ours be driven much longer we shall lose a great part of the Bark for I have Observed for years back that Old Hedge rows goes best in the first bud.

[1] Hampson, 'History of Heath'.
[2] Nottingham University, MaB 347/59.

I am Sir, your most Obedient Humble Servant.

*T. Greaves.*

In July of that year a note was made: 'To carriage of 2 ton 15 cwt of coals from Oldcotes Pit to Thoresby at 14s. per ton £1 18s. 10d.' Also in 1802 there is a letter from Thomas Greaves the elder to the agent at Thoresby regarding a wrong account for coals mined at Oldcotes Pit.[1]

The earliest record of a tenant farmer at Oldcotes appears to be Thomas Greaves the elder. Unfortunately, there is no means of knowing when he became tenant. Heath parish registers are incomplete, and the first entry relating to the family records the baptism of their second son in 1763, so presumably he came to Oldcotes as a young married man with a son Thomas in about 1760. From 1763 he took a prominent part in the life of the parish. He was church-warden in 1765, 1766, 1772 and in 1779, when Heath church steeple was rebuilt; in 1785, when his first wife Ann died aged 54, by whom he had seven children; and in 1791. He was surveyor of highways in 1766 and overseer of the poor in 1765, 1771, 1772, 1779 and 1784. He remarried in 1786 Ann Hurt of High House. He was then 54, and it was at this time he moved over to High House and became involved in the sinking and subsequent working of Oldcotes Pit.

Thomas Greaves the younger married Ann Chawner of Heath and occupied two cottages adjoining Summer House Close, with a croft to one of them. When his father moved to High House he moved into Oldcotes where there was a large farmhouse, outbuildings, yard, garden and barn close, plus 294 acres of land which had previously been farmed by himself and his father.

Thomas Greaves the elder made his will in 1803[2] and died in 1805 aged 73. To his son Thomas Greaves of Oldcotes, farmer, he bequeathed the tenant right of his farm which he held under Lord Newark, together with all his stock thereon quick as well as dead, his implements of husbandry, goods, chattels, money and effects and personal estate, on trust that his son make an inventory, so that no waste might be committed of the same during the lifetime of 'my dear wife Ann', who was to be allowed to live at High House during her widowhood and have the profits of the farm. Should Ann decide not to remain there, his son was to allow her to take for her own benefit any bed of her choice and enough furniture for one room, and she was to receive an annuity of £25 for as long as she remained a widow, or £10 should she remarry. If Ann left the farm, remarried or died, his son Thomas was to sell all the stock then on High

[1] Nottingham University, MaB 355/13.
[2] Lichfield Record Office.

House Farm, quick and dead, and all implements of husbandry, goods, chattels, effects and personal estate, and with the money pay annuities to the testator's son Samuel Greaves (£30) and daughter Sarah Denham, the wife of Job Denham (£20). The residue from the sale, together with such part of his personal estate as consisted of money at the time of his decease, was to be equally divided amongst his surviving sons and daughters, Thomas Greaves, Samuel Greaves, Dorothy the wife of Nathaniel Bacon, and Sarah Denham, share and share alike. Should his daughter Dorothy happen to be dead (she died in 1805), then her share to be equally divided amongst her children, and in such a manner as his son Thomas thought most fit for their advancement in the world. He appointed his son Thomas his sole executor.

The will was witnessed by Robert Waller, then Chesterfield's leading attorney, and John March, the schoolmaster and parish clerk of Sutton-cum-Duckmanton, who probably wrote it. Probate was granted at Chesterfield on 24 April 1806, Thomas Greaves jun. duly swearing that his father's estate was not above the value of £1,000. Thomas's wife Ann died in December 1792 aged 32, and Thomas made the journey on horseback to Lichfield on 1 January 1793 to testify that she had died 'upwards of fourteen days since'; that she had died intestate and that he was the person entitled to letters of administration of her goods and personal estate; and that they did not exceed £100.[1]

He remarried on 14 November 1796 Margaret Johnson, spinster, of the Angel Inn, Chesterfield. The marriage was by special licence at Chesterfield church; he was 35 and Margaret 31. Miss Johnson was one of the old coaching landladies of Chesterfield. The Post Office and National Westminster Bank in the Market Place have absorbed between them the site of the Angel. The inn was approached under an archway, and up the Angel Yard was a small room which at one time still bore over the door the title 'Coach Office'. The stables and coach houses stretched as far back as Saltergate. Up the stairs was a large room, long used as a Freemansons' Hall. Miss Johnson was not only the landlady, but also the owner of the property. When she married and went to live at Oldcotes, she left the Angel under the management of Thomas Evison. The most important inn in Chesterfield, it remained a great coaching house until the North Midland Railway was opened in 1840.

Thomas and Margaret had four children: William born in 1797, Margaret in 1799, Thomas in 1801 and Sarah in 1805. In 1803 a survey of Oldcotes was made for Viscount Newark, when it was valued at £300 9s. 8d. When her husband Thomas died in 1825 at the age of 64, Margaret was to prove that she was as capable a farmer as she had been a landlady. Thomas left her the remaining

---

[1] Lichfield Record Office.

**Figure 21** The Angel Inn on the north side of the Market Place, Chesterfield.

years of his lease of Oldcotes and, with the help of her two sons and daughter Margaret, she became a successful farmer in her own right of 280 acres. Their marriage had obviously been a happy one, as Thomas referred to her throughout his will as his 'dear wife', leaving her the entire contents of Oldcotes and all his farming stock and gear, and making her his sole executrix. If she remarried, or at her death, then everything was to be shared equally between their four children. Should Margaret die before the expiration of the farm lease, then he bequeathed this to their eldest son William.[1] Thomas Greaves jun., like his father before him, had been prominent in local affairs. He was churchwarden in 1793 and 1799, and overseer of the poor in 1793, 1803 and 1819.

Margaret Greaves farmed Oldcotes from the time of her husband's death in 1825 to her own death in 1847. In 1826 it was proposed to enclose the common land in the manor of Stainsby and Heath and the following notice was issued:

[1] Lichfield Record Office, will of Thomas Greaves jun.

The proprietors of the Estates within the Manor of STAINSBY and HEATH in the Parishes of Ault Hucknall and Heath in the County of Derby will hold a meeting at Mr Goodwin's the sign of the ELM TREE, in HEATH, on Friday, the 8th day of December next at 11 o'clock in the Forenoon and take into consideration the means of effecting a GENERAL INCLOSURE of the COMMONS and WASTE GROUND within the said Manor, at which meeting a CONSENT BILL for accomplishing the same will be produced and read and when all persons interested are desired to attend.

Chesterfield 23rd Nov. 1826

By Order
John Charge
Solicitor, Chesterfield

According to the Act which was obtained the following year, there was 90 acres of common pasture belonging to the manor in the parish of Heath. On 30 June 1827 the following notice was published in the local paper:

All claims delivered in by any person claiming to be entitled to Right of Common under the above enclosure—a book wherein entry is made of all claims delivered in—now lying at the house of Mr Goodwin, the sign of the Elm Tree, and another at Mr Sampson Clay's, the sign of the Shoulder of Mutton (Hardstoft).

Claims relating to common rights were received from the Oldcotes tenants:

Mr Hurt tenant of High House 1777, had sheep on Heath Common, Mr Joseph Armstrong lived there and worked for him.
John Armstrong now occupies the Cottage upon Old cotes Farm and has done so for the past 34 years—and has during that period stocked the Common with 4 Sheep, Asses, Pigs and Geese.
Matthew Fox, who died a year ago aged 80 and upwards, lived in the house adjoining Armstrong—he constantly turned Sheep and Lambs to the time of his death, so long back as Armstrong can recollect.
Owing to the death of the Old Tenants of the Old cotes Farms, Mr Pickin (agent) cannot show evidence of their stocking the Commons. The present Tenant of High House, Mr H. Goodwin, rents Farm and Common rights, House, of the Duke of Devonshire, and therefore his stocking of the Common being so small a piece of land, it is reasonable to presume that the farmers might not think it worth while to turn

cattle upon it, and it has actually been the case that the Common has been more stocked by Cottagers than Farmers.

Between 1834 and 1838 it appears the Oldcotes park trees were sold as the sale of the timber is recorded:

1834. Mr Cocking engaging to pay £220 for timber sold to him from Owlcotes.

| | |
|---|---|
| Charles Whitworth sale of | 755 feet of ash timber at 1/6d. per foot. |
| | 19 poles at 1/6d. each |
| Mrs Lamb | 710 feet of ash 1/3d. per foot. |
| | 30 poles at 1/3d. each. |
| Jes. Thompson | 99 feet of Elm timber at 1/3d. per foot. |
| | 25 feet of Ash at 1/3d. per foot. |
| Jos. Bennett | 100 feet of Alder at 1/8d. per foot. |
| | 14 stronger Alder poles at 5d. each. |
| | 30 small Alder at 1d. each. |

The 1841 census lists Margaret Greaves, a farmer aged 76, sons William and Thomas, also farmers, aged 44 and 40 respectively, and daughter Margaret, 42 and single, at Oldcotes. Sarah, the youngest daughter, was visiting, along with her three children, for Sarah had married a Mr Cawton, a tanner of Baslow. Employed in the house and upon the farm were two maidservants and three male labourers. In October 1845 William Greaves died a bachelor aged 48, and in October 1846 his sister Sarah, by then a widow, remarried Robert Platts, a veterinary surgeon from Killamarsh. The following month sister Margaret married Joseph Brailsford, a widower and licensed vitualler in Chesterfield.

In 1847 Margaret Greaves died aged 82. At the time of her death, she was paying a half-yearly rent of £241 for Oldcotes, which consisted of 280 acres of land, a house, farmyard, garden, stabling for 6/7 horses, a large barn with two threshing floors, hay barn, cowsheds, pig cotes and malting house. She made her will in 1846[1] and it is interesting to note that at the time of her death she was still the owner of the Angel in Chesterfield. She gave and devised to Job Denham, butcher of Heath, and Charles Cawton, tanner of Baslow, to hold on trust the Angel Inn, in the Market Place, Chesterfield, together with the yard, stables, coach houses and outbuildings, allowing her son Thomas Greaves, the rents and profits during his natural life. After his death the Angel Inn and its

[1] Lichfield Record Office.

**Figure 22** A *carte de visite* view of Owlcotes by the leading late 19th-century Derby photographer, Richard Keene.

premises went to be sold, the money invested, and the income therefrom held in trust for the three children of her daughter Sarah Cawton, in equal shares. Should they die before reaching the age of 21, then the proceeds were to go to her son Thomas Greaves and his heirs. Should her son Thomas Greaves so desire, he might sell the inn and enjoy the profits during his lifetime. To her daughter Margaret she left two dwelling houses in St Mary's Gate, Chesterfield (otherwise Lordsmill Street). To Job Denham and her son Thomas Greaves she left £1,400 to be invested and the annual income to be paid to Sarah Cawton during her lifetime, and afterwards to her three children when they reached the age of 21. The trustees were allowed to raise any part of the expected share if necessary for the benefit or the advancement or education of the children. In accordance with her husband's wishes she left her surviving children, Thomas, Margaret and Sarah, in equal shares, the household goods, furniture, plate, linen, china, farm stock, cattle, chattels, crops, personal estate and effects. To her son Thomas Greaves, she left her tenant rights to Owlcotes farm which she held under Earl Manvers, trusting he would accept her son Thomas as tenant.

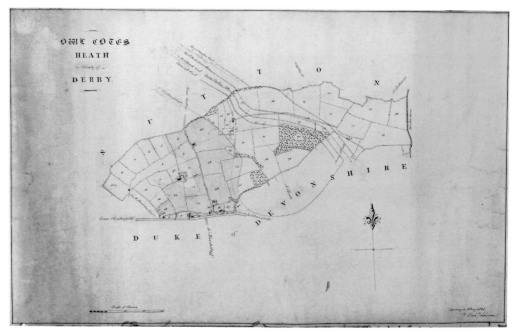

**Figure 23** Plan of the Owlcotes estate by Richard Johnson, 1861, showing the farmsteads at Owlcotes and High House and the outcrop of several coal seams.

Thomas, on taking over the farm, was to share the tillage and growing crops for that year with his sisters. The residue of her real estate she left to her daughter Margaret. Her signature was witnessed by Samuel Johnson (a relative) and Joseph Shipton (the Chesterfield solicitor).

In the disused churchyard of All Saints, Heath, is a gravestone:

> In memory of Thomas Greaves who departed this life January 20th 1825 aged 64 years. Also Margaret widow of the above Thomas Greaves who departed this life Nov. 23rd 1847 aged 82 years. William son of Thomas and Margaret Greaves who departed this life Oct. 27th 1845 aged 48 years.

Nearby is another stone bearing the following inscription:

> This stone is erected in the memory of Thomas Brailsford who departed this life on the 1st May 1823 aged 75 years. Late servant to Mr Greaves (of Old Cotes) he lived respected and died there lamented by the family.

> Whilst in this world he did remain,
> He was afflicted with much pain,
> With patience to the end he did submit,

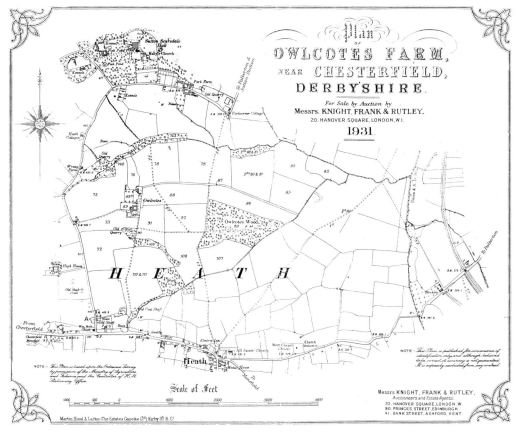

**Figure 24** Owlcotes Farm, from the sale catalogue of 1931.

> He murmur'd not at what the Lord thought fit,
> Himself to God he did resign,
> Unto the Lord at His appointed time.

Earl Manvers accepted Margaret's son Thomas Greaves into the remaining years of her lease. Thomas had married in 1847 Ann Rome, whose father James Rome kept the Elm Tree Inn at Heath. In 1851 Thomas was farming 200 acres at Owlcotes and they had a son Thomas aged one. He employed three agricultural workers and two servant girls to assist in the house. Four more children were born to them at Owlcotes. At the same time Thomas sold the Angel Inn, for we find that in the 1850s, after the coming of the railways to Chesterfield, the Angel was in the ownership of the Evison family.

This Thomas Greaves was the last member of the family to farm at Owlcotes. Perhaps the condition of the premises may have influenced his decision, for as early as 1840 and again in 1848 the family were complaining to the agent about the condition of the house, which was old, large and inconvenient. The reply was that the estate was unwilling to spend money on a new house, which would cost every penny of £1,000. On Shire Lane were two cottages both occupied by Owlcotes labourers who were married with families, and there was a third cottage also occupied by an Owlcotes labourer.

By 1881 William Wetton was farming 282 acres at Owlcotes. He and his wife Lydia had a family of two boys and a girl. He employed three farm labourers and a servant girl. A well-known breeder of White Wine-Dot fowls, he was still there in the early 1900s.

Returning to High House, Humphrey Goodwin of Heath married Elizabeth Hill, also of Heath, in 1792. He is understood to have built the Elm Tree Inn in 1808 and to have kept the inn until 1826. He was also a farmer of 109 acres. It was at the inn that their ten children were born, three dying very young. His wife Elizabeth died in 1818 while they were still running the inn. In 1827 he left the inn to take over High House farm and the coalpit. His daughter Ann kept house for him after her mother's death. Regrettably no records have survived concerning his farming and mining activities, but he was a well-to-do farmer, prominent in the village, where he was churchwarden from 1808 to 1828.

In 1842, a year before Humphrey Goodwin's death, the Children's Employment Commissioner wrote, after visiting Oldcotes Pit:

> Charles John Goodwin is son of H. Goodwin. His father has only two shafts both of them are worked by gin-horses and are 30 yards deep. They employ no children except the gin-horse drivers, one 10 years and the other 12, and only one young man aged 15 years old. They work from 7 to 6 for whole days but seldom make them as the pits are very small dependant on Land Sale.

Here we have a prime example of the local employment of child labour, when a full day's labour entailed 11 working hours. According to *Bagshaw's Derbyshire Directory* (1846), Oldcotes was an extensive colliery, mining excellent coal and having a good road leading to the turnpike road. In the 1841 Census High House who occupied by Humphrey Goodwin, aged 72, and Ann his daughter, aged 45; he was employing two farm labourers and two female servants. He died two years later, and was buried with his wife in the old churchyard at Heath, where an inscription reads: 'Sacred to the memory of Humphrey Goodwin who departed this life June 13th 1843 in the 74th year of his age. Sacred to the memory of Elizabeth, wife of Humphrey Goodwin who departed this life June 19th 1818 in the 50th year of her age'.

**Figure 25** Owlcotes in 1964.

In his will[1] Humphrey Goodwin bequeathed to his three surviving sons, William, George and Charles John, all his personal estate, share and share alike. To his daughter Anne he left £22 and an annuity of £20; to Mary, the wife of John Brockmer, £20 a year for life; to Betsy, the wife of Job Denham, £500. To Charlotte, the wife of John Collier, £25 a year for life and in the case of her death the same to her husband for life, and after his decease and that of his wife, £500 to be equally divided between their children. To his three sons he left 'the possession and tenant right of the Colliery I hold of the Rt. Hon. Earl Manvers at Old Cotes to hold and carry on the same and also the Colliery I have at Birchwood', jointly in equal shares for their mutual benefit. To his son George he left the possession and tenant right of the farm at High House which he also held of Manvers. To his son Charles John he left the possession and tenant right of the farm at Blackwell which he held of the Earl of Carnarvon. His son George Goodwin to have the household furniture, farming stock and crops at High House, and Charles the same at Blackwell. All three sons were appointed executors.

George Goodwin succeeded his father as tenant at High House. He shared the tenant right to Oldcotes Pit with his two brothers William and Charles John. According to the 1851 Census George Goodwin was aged 39, his wife Harriet

[1] Lichfield Record Office.

93

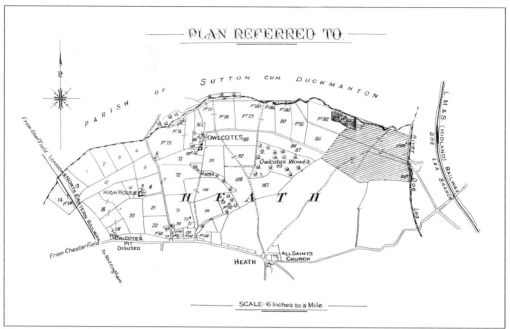

**Figure 26** Plan of the Owlcotes estate, 1928. Note the disused Owlcotes Pit, a small landsale colliery on the Chesterfield Road near High House.

aged 28, and they had two children, George aged four and Mary aged five. George was farming 140 acres and employed two agricultural labourers and two female servants.

High House is missing from the 1861 Census. However, *White's Derbyshire Directory* (1862) lists William Goodwin as a farmer there, but he had left before 1871, the last of his family to farm at High House. William died in 1874, as a stone in Heath churchyard records:

> Sacred to the memory of William Goodwin born at Heath, April 2nd 1810, died at Chesterfield Feb. 21st 1874 aged 64. Also Martha his wife who departed this life June 13th 1885. Looking unto Jesus.

Charles John Goodwin, the youngest of the brothers, was listed as 'Farmer and Innkeeper' when his children were baptised at Heath between 1830 and 1844, the eldest son being named William Galloway Goodwin. In 1862 *White's Directory* lists Galloway & Co. as the occupiers of Owlcotes Colliery, with John Brockmer (who had married Mary Goodwin in 1832) as manager, presumably indicating that the business had passed to other members of the family. In 1928 the Manvers estate sold the pit, which by this date was disused, together with the coal underlying the whole of their Owlcotes property (which they had

94

reserved in the sale of 1910), to the Hardwick Colliery Co. Ltd.[1]

In the 1871 Census Edward Robinson and his wife Mary, aged 39 and 41 respectively, and their seven children aged from 13 years to two months, were at High House, having come from Ockbrook to farm 127 acres. They employed one agricultural worker and one female servant. The same family was in residence in 1881, when the farm was 130 acres. The 1891 Census shows a change in tenancy to James Roberts, aged 45, his wife Jane, aged 47, and their three children. This family came to High House from Brimington and employed two male agricultural workers. They remained at High House until after 1900.

The twentieth century has seen great changes in farming and farming methods. The horse, for centuries a vital part of farming life, gradually gave way to the tractor and other mechanical aids to successful farming, replacing the need to employ so many labourers. Many small farms became absorbed into larger concerns, hedges were removed, field acreage increased, and bird-life diminished, but mercifully Owlcotes and High House with their lands have remained to continue into the new Millennium. Hedges may have been removed and fields made larger; the names of the fields may have changed, as has the nature of their farming. Nevertheless, if those early occupiers of the two farms were to pass this way again, they would still be able to recognises their old homesteads, after almost three hundred years.

It would be possible to continue the list of tenant farmers at Oldcotes and High House until both became owner-occupied. Sufficient to say that Owlcotes Farm is today the property of Mr John Mower, and High House Farm that of Mr Eric Taylor. Neither is open to the public.

---

[1] Nottingham University, Manvers MS 3294.